Carry the Torch &

THE AZRIELI SERIES OF HOLOCAUST SURVIVOR MEMOIRS: PUBLISHED TITLES

ENGLISH TITLES

Judy Abrams, *Tenuous Threads*/ Eva Felsenburg Marx, *One of the Lucky Ones*
Amek Adler, *Six Lost Years*
Molly Applebaum, *Buried Words*
Claire Baum, *The Hidden Package*
Tibor Benyovits, *Unsung Heroes*
Bronia and Joseph Beker, *Joy Runs Deeper*
Max Bornstein, *If Home Is Not Here*
Felicia Carmelly, *Across the Rivers of Memory*
Tommy Dick, *Getting Out Alive*
Marian Domanski, *Fleeing from the Hunter*
John Freund, *Spring's End*
Myrna Goldenberg (Editor), *Before All Memory Is Lost: Women's Voices from the Holocaust*
René Goldman, *A Childhood Adrift*
Ibolya Grossman and Andy Réti, *Stronger Together*
Pinchas Gutter, *Memories in Focus*
Anna Molnár Hegedűs, *As the Lilacs Bloomed*
Rabbi Pinchas Hirschprung, *The Vale of Tears*
Bronia Jablon, *A Part of Me*
Helena Jockel, *We Sang in Hushed Voices*
Eddie Klein, *Inside the Walls*
Michael Kutz, *If, By Miracle*
Nate Leipciger, *The Weight of Freedom*
Alex Levin, *Under the Yellow and Red Stars*
Fred Mann, *A Drastic Turn of Destiny*
Michael Mason, *A Name Unbroken*
Leslie Meisels with Eva Meisels, *Suddenly the Shadow Fell*

Muguette Myers, *Where Courage Lives*
David Newman, *Hope's Reprise*
Arthur Ney, *W Hour*
Felix Opatowski, *Gatehouse to Hell*
Marguerite Élias Quddus, *In Hiding*
Maya Rakitova, *Behind the Red Curtain*
Henia Reinhartz, *Bits and Pieces*
Betty Rich, *Little Girl Lost*
Paul-Henri Rips, *E/96: Fate Undecided*
Margrit Rosenberg Stenge, *Silent Refuge*
Steve Rotschild, *Traces of What Was*
Judith Rubinstein, *Dignity Endures*
Kitty Salsberg and Ellen Foster, *Never Far Apart*
Zuzana Sermer, *Survival Kit*
Rachel Shtibel, *The Violin*/ Adam Shtibel, *A Child's Testimony*
Maxwell Smart, *Chaos to Canvas*
Gerta Solan, *My Heart Is At Ease*
Zsuzsanna Fischer Spiro, *In Fragile Moments*/ Eva Shainblum, *The Last Time*
George Stern, *Vanished Boyhood*
Willie Sterner, *The Shadows Behind Me*
Ann Szedlecki, *Album of My Life*
William Tannenzapf, *Memories from the Abyss*/ Renate Krakauer, *But I Had a Happy Childhood*
Elsa Thon, *If Only It Were Fiction*
Agnes Tomasov, *From Generation to Generation*
Joseph Tomasov, *From Loss to Liberation*
Leslie Vertes, *Alone in the Storm*
Anka Voticky, *Knocking on Every Door*

TITRES FRANÇAIS

Judy Abrams, *Retenue par un fil*/ Eva Felsenburg Marx, *Une question de chance*
Claire Baum, *Le Colis caché*
Bronia et Joseph Beker, *Plus forts que le malheur*
Max Bornstein, *Citoyen de nulle part*
Tommy Dick, *Objectif: survivre*
Marian Domanski, *Traqué*
John Freund, *La Fin du printemps*
René Goldman, *Une enfance à la dérive*
Anna Molnár Hegedűs, *Pendant la saison des lilas*
Helena Jockel, *Nous chantions en sourdine*
Michael Kutz, *Si, par miracle*
Nate Leipciger, *Le Poids de la liberté*
Alex Levin, *Étoile jaune, étoile rouge*
Fred Mann, *Un terrible revers de fortune*
Michael Mason, *Au fil d'un nom*
Leslie Meisels, *Soudains, les ténèbres*
Muguette Myers, *Les Lieux du courage*
Arthur Ney, *L'Heure W*

Felix Opatowski, *L'Antichambre de l'enfer*
Marguerite Élias Quddus, *Cachée*
Henia Reinhartz, *Fragments de ma vie*
Betty Rich, *Seule au monde*
Paul-Henri Rips, *Matricule E/96*
Steve Rotschild, *Sur les traces du passé*
Kitty Salsberg et Ellen Foster, *Unies dans l'épreuve*
Zuzana Sermer, *Trousse de survie*
Rachel Shtibel, *Le Violon*/ Adam Shtibel, *Témoignage d'un enfant*
George Stern, *Une jeunesse perdue*
Willie Sterner, *Les Ombres du passé*
Ann Szedlecki, *L'Album de ma vie*
William Tannenzapf, *Souvenirs de l'abîme*/ Renate Krakauer, *Le Bonheur de l'innocence*
Elsa Thon, *Que renaisse demain*
Agnes Tomasov, *De génération en génération*
Leslie Vertes, *Seul dans la tourmente*
Anka Voticky, *Frapper à toutes les portes*

Carry the Torch
Sam Weisberg

A Lasting Legacy
Johnny Jablon

FIRST EDITION
Copyright © 2018 The Azrieli Foundation and others

All rights reserved

Copyright in individual works, parts of works and/or photographs included within this published work is also claimed by individuals and entities. All requests and questions concerning copyright and reproduction of all or part of this publication may be directed to The Azrieli Foundation.

THE AZRIELI FOUNDATION
www.azrielifoundation.org

Cover and book design by Mark Goldstein. Endpaper maps by Martin Gilbert. Maps on page xxix by François Blanc. Documents on page 194 courtesy of International Tracing Service (ITS) Bad Arolsen. Top photo on page 206 courtesy Naomi Wise. Bottom photo on page 206 and photos on page 207 courtesy PBL Photography.

LIBRARY AND ARCHIVES CANADA CATALOGUING IN PUBLICATION

Carry the torch/ Sam Weisberg; A lasting legacy/ Johnny Jablon.

(Azrieli series of Holocaust survivor memoirs. Series x)
Includes bibliographical references and index.
ISBN 978-1-988065-46-5 (softcover) · 8 7 6 5 4 3 2 1

1. Weisberg, Sam, 1927–. 2. Jablon, Johnny, 1926–. 3. Holocaust, Jewish (1939–1945). 4. Holocaust survivors — Canada — Biography. 5. Jews — Canada — Biography. 6. Autobiographies. I. Azrieli Foundation, issuing body. II. Weisberg, Sam, 1927–. Carry the torch. III. Jablon, Johnny, 1926–. Lasting legacy. IV. Title: Lasting legacy. V. Series: Azrieli series of Holocaust survivor memoirs. Series x.

FC106.J5C4285 2018   940.53'18092271   C2018-906080-8

MIX
From responsible sources
FSC® C004191

PRINTED IN CANADA

The Azrieli Series of Holocaust Survivor Memoirs

Naomi Azrieli, Publisher

Jody Spiegel, Program Director
Arielle Berger, Managing Editor
Matt Carrington, Editor
Devora Levin, Assistant Editor
Elizabeth Lasserre, Senior Editor, French-Language Editions
Elin Beaumont, Senior Education Outreach and Program Facilitator
Catherine Person, Bilingual Education and Outreach Coordinator
Stephanie Corazza, Education and Curriculum Associate
Marc-Olivier Cloutier, Bilingual Educational Outreach and Events Assistant
Elizabeth Banks, Digital Asset Curator and Archivist
Susan Roitman, Office Manager (Toronto)
Mary Mellas, Executive Assistant and Human Resources (Montreal)

Mark Goldstein, Art Director
François Blanc, Cartographer
Bruno Paradis, Layout, French-Language Editions

Contents

Series Preface	xi
About the Glossary	xiii
Introduction *by Joanna Sliwa*	xv
Maps	xxix

SAM WEISBERG

Polish Roots	5
Crossing Borders	17
To the Other Side	27
The Start of Terror	33
Speaking Up	45
Rebirth	53
Strength to Endure	59
New Names, New World	69
A Bar Mitzvah Abroad	79
Epilogue	83

JOHNNY JABLON

Preface	87
What I Remember	89
The Horror of the Camps	97
The Luck of Selection	103

Staying Alive	111
Like Ghosts on the Move	119
Freedom!	121
Building a Home in a Camp	127
Canada and the Road to Happiness	131
Becoming a Family	145
I Found My Revenge	147
Glossary	153
Photographs	171
Index	211

Series Preface:
In their own words...

In telling these stories, the writers have liberated themselves. For so many years we did not speak about it, even when we became free people living in a free society. Now, when at last we are writing about what happened to us in this dark period of history, knowing that our stories will be read and live on, it is possible for us to feel truly free. These unique historical documents put a face on what was lost, and allow readers to grasp the enormity of what happened to six million Jews — one story at a time.

>David J. Azrieli, C.M., C.Q., M.Arch
>Holocaust survivor and founder, The Azrieli Foundation

Since the end of World War II, approximately 40,000 Jewish Holocaust survivors have immigrated to Canada. Who they are, where they came from, what they experienced and how they built new lives for themselves and their families are important parts of our Canadian heritage. The Azrieli Foundation's Holocaust Survivor Memoirs Program was established in 2005 to preserve and share the memoirs written by those who survived the twentieth-century Nazi genocide of the Jews of Europe and later made their way to Canada. The program is guided by the conviction that each survivor of the Holocaust has a remarkable story to tell, and that such stories play an important role in education about tolerance and diversity.

Millions of individual stories are lost to us forever. By preserving the stories written by survivors and making them widely available to a broad audience, the Azrieli Foundation's Holocaust Survivor Memoirs Program seeks to sustain the memory of all those who perished at the hands of hatred, abetted by indifference and apathy. The personal accounts of those who survived against all odds are as different as the people who wrote them, but all demonstrate the courage, strength, wit and luck that it took to prevail and survive in such terrible adversity. The memoirs are also moving tributes to people — strangers and friends — who risked their lives to help others, and who, through acts of kindness and decency in the darkest of moments, frequently helped the persecuted maintain faith in humanity and courage to endure. These accounts offer inspiration to all, as does the survivors' desire to share their experiences so that new generations can learn from them.

The Holocaust Survivor Memoirs Program collects, archives and publishes select survivor memoirs and makes the print editions available free of charge to educational institutions and Holocaust-education programs across Canada. They are also available for sale to the general public at bookstores. All revenues to the Azrieli Foundation from the sales of the Azrieli Series of Holocaust Survivor Memoirs go toward the publishing and educational work of the memoirs program.

∼

The Azrieli Foundation would like to express appreciation to the following people for their invaluable efforts in producing this book: Doris Bergen, Sherry Dodson (Maracle Inc), Helen Guri, Myrna Riback and Maxine Silverman, Jane Pavanel, Therese Parent, and Margie Wolfe & Emma Rodgers of Second Story Press.

About the Glossary

The following memoir contains a number of terms, concepts and historical references that may be unfamiliar to the reader. For information on major organizations; significant historical events and people; geographical locations; religious and cultural terms; and foreign-language words and expressions that will help give context and background to the events described in the text, please see the glossary beginning on page 153.

Introduction

Sam Weisberg (born Avraham Ichak Gajer) and Ephroim (Johnny) Jablon (born Jan Rothbaum) were part of the first generation in over a century to live in an independent Poland. Both came from Jewish families rooted in Krakow. The city, which Jews referred to as the "Jerusalem of Galicia,"[1] served as an important historical, religious and cultural centre. Once a royal town and the capital of Poland, Krakow attracted merchants, intellectuals and artists. Dotted with Jewish prayer houses of different denominations, strewn with a well-developed network of community-supported institutions, and filled with cultural, educational and political endeavours, Krakow offered a thriving Jewish life.[2] According to the pre-World War II Polish census of 1931, Krakow had the fourth largest Jewish population in Poland after Warsaw, Lodz and Lwów. This largely acculturated and Polish-speaking Jewish community of 56,000 people comprised about 25 per cent of Krakow's population.

---

1 Galicia was the name given to the easternmost administrative region of Austria-Hungary following the partitions of the First Polish Republic among Austria, Prussia and Russia in the eighteenth century. For an overview of its history, see Larry Wolff, *The Idea of Galicia: History and Fantasy in Habsburg Political Culture* (Stanford, CA: Stanford University Press, 2012).
2 For a study on Jewish life in Krakow in the interwar period, see Sean Martin, *Jewish Life in Cracow, 1918–1939* (London; Portland, OR: Vallentine Mitchell, 2004).

This was the environment in which Johnny grew up and one that shaped Sam's upbringing, as both of Sam's parents were Krakovians. Sam was raised in Chorzów, in western Poland, a city less than one hundred kilometres from Krakow. Sam's parents settled there after they had returned from British Mandate Palestine, where they had immigrated in the 1920s. Economic difficulties, inability to adapt to the local climate and lack of family networks were some reasons why immigrants, such as Sam's parents, went back to their countries of origin. By then, Chorzów, known for its mines and industry, had been transferred from Germany to Poland. Yet the German culture and language continued to influence the city and its residents, so much so that Sam learned German from his non-Jewish German nanny and spoke it better than Polish, the language of instruction at his Jewish day school.

In the latter part of the 1930s, the atmosphere for Jews in Chorzów thickened. Jewish refugees from Germany, many of whom were former residents, arrived in the city and informed local Jews about the deteriorating situation across the border. Sam's parents decided it would be safer to move to Krakow. Still, neither Sam's nor Johnny's families, or other Jews in Krakow for that matter, expected the worst. In summer 1939, both Sam and Johnny, like many other Jewish and non-Jewish children, departed for their vacation in the Polish mountains. Rumours about an imminent war forced each boy to return home early. Their carefree childhoods were cut short by the outbreak of World War II.

The decisions made by Sam's and Johnny's parents mirrored those of thousands of other Jews from Krakow in the face of uncertainty that the war carried. Fearing the approaching German army, some Jews fled eastward, among them Sam and his family. Sam was trapped when the Soviet Union invaded Poland on September 17, 1939, according to the pact that it had signed just a month earlier with Nazi Germany. Poland was divided between the two superpowers roughly along the Bug River. Hoping for better treatment from the Soviets than they would receive from the Germans, Sam's family moved to Lwów, then under Soviet control.[3] When the Soviet regime deported foreigners who refused to accept Soviet citizenship and those it deemed enemies, Sam's aunt, uncle and their two sons were forcibly shipped to Siberia. Sam and his parents were spared. Paradoxically, the deportees evaded German occupation. Those left in Lwów, on the other hand, endured a different fate. Sam's memoir throws light on the various forms of persecution that Jews experienced and on their coping strategies under each regime.

On June 22, 1941, Germany invaded the Soviet Union, capturing Lwów just eight days later. A two-day pogrom erupted in which Ukrainian nationalists supported by German Einsatzgruppen (mobile killing squads that accompanied the German army) publicly humiliated Jews and murdered up to five thousand. Jews were unjustly accused of having sided with the detested Soviet regime and were blamed for its atrocities against the Ukrainian and Polish ethnic populations. Terror reigned in the city. Lwów became the capital of District Galicia, one of five German-created districts — in addition to Krakow, Lublin, Radom and Warsaw — that were part of the General Government, a German administrative area of occupied Poland.[4] Rumours about the creation of a ghetto circulated.[5] Sam's mother had no illusions about what awaited them under German

---

3 The city was renamed Lvov. For information on the Soviet and German occupations of Lwów, see Christopher Mick, *Lemberg, Lwów, Lviv, 1914–1947: Violence and Ethnicity in a Contested City* (West Lafayette, IN: Purdue University Press, 2015).
4 In his study, *The Dark Heart of Hitler's Europe: Nazi Rule in Poland under the General Government* (New York: I.B. Tauris & Co., 2015), Martin Winstone examined the roles of the General Government in the Nazi scheme of reordering Europe: as a dumping ground for unwanted peoples, site of exploitation and place of murder.
5 A ghetto was created in November 1941. In the course of German actions in the ghetto, Jews were deported to the Bełżec killing centre, while others were assigned to forced labour inside the ghetto and in the nearby Janowska camp.

occupation. She preferred to be close to her extended family, and Sam and his parents were smuggled back to the place they had left less than two years earlier.

Much had changed in Krakow since 1939. Johnny, who remained in the city like most Krakow Jews, endured these shifts. Interestingly, he does not devote much attention in his memoir to his life prior to the creation of the ghetto. Perhaps those events faded in comparison to his suffering in the ghetto and later in the camps. Then too, he was still a young boy of thirteen when the German regime refashioned Krakow into the capital of the General Government and the seat of Krakow District. Because Nazi ideology considered Krakow inherently Germanic, the city was not bombed like Warsaw, Poland's prewar capital. Instead, Krakow was to serve as a model German city in the East. But what was to be done with the city's Jews? On September 8, two days after the German army occupied Krakow, the German administration ordered the creation of a Jewish Council (Judenrat) that received German orders and was responsible for executing Jews' compliance with them. The Jewish Council had other duties: drafting forced labourers, registering the Jewish population and providing welfare and medical services for Jews of all ages. According to a census conducted in November 1939, there were over 46,000 Jewish adults and close to 19,000 Jewish children up to the age of sixteen in Krakow and the surrounding areas.

The German authorities did not wish to accommodate Jews in the city. Their goal was to control and remove them. In December 1939, Jews above the age of twelve were ordered to display a white armband with a blue Star of David. Jews were now branded, and their every move was monitored. Restrictions on movement introduced in May 1940 defined where Jewish presence was prohibited, thereby forcing Jews to leave their homes and move to the Jewish quarter in the Kazimierz district. That same month, a German decree ordered the expulsion of Jews from the city. This was quite an unusual measure, but it aligned with Nazi plans to transform Polish Krakow into German Krakau (the city's name was formally Germanized in August 1941). A Jewish Order Service (Jüdischer Ordnungsdienst, OD, also referred to as the Jewish police) was created in the summer of 1940 to assist the Jewish Council with the onerous task imposed on it by the German regime to prepare the deportations, deliver and enforce German regulations, and maintain order in the Jewish district. By November 1940, some 20,000 Jews remained in Krakow, including those who had received permission to stay and those who were living there illegally.

While Johnny and his family were allowed to stay in Krakow, the expellees had to move to villages and towns on the outskirts of the city or to other localities within the General Government. But on March 3, 1941, the Jews of Krakow suffered another blow — a law establishing a Jewish residential district, which was nothing but a ghetto, a site where Jews were confined and forced to live under immense restrictions. The ghetto was located not in Kazimierz, but across the Vistula River, in Podgórze. Again, in quite an unusual measure, Jews deemed adults by German law (meaning those over the age of fourteen) were required to obtain permission from the German authorities to enter the ghetto. Over 16,000 Jews applied, but only about 11,000 were approved. Those rejected, as well as those who decided not to apply, left the city. It was only on June 1, 1941, that the German authorities incorporated twenty-seven localities into Krakow and forced their Jewish inhabitants, many of them former expellees, to move to the Krakow ghetto in late summer and early fall 1941.

The Germans imposed different restrictions on the categories of Jews eligible to enter the Krakow ghetto and this influenced the fate of Sam and his parents, who were en route to Krakow from Lwów in June 1941. The family had to make a swift decision, and they headed instead to Wieliczka, a town about fifteen kilometres from their destination, where Sam's mother had a relative. She soon learned that her sisters, who had been expelled from Krakow, had settled in the town of Wolbrom, about seventy kilometres northwest of Wieliczka.[6] That is where Sam and his parents travelled. There, they lived in the town's open ghetto, created just a month prior to their arrival. The German authorities designated an area near the synagogue where Jews were permitted to live. No physical structures separated the ghetto from the rest of the town. This arrangement differed from the ghetto in Krakow, where walls, barbed wire, gates and bricked-up windows and doors overlooking the "Aryan" (non-Jewish) side delineated its borders. Sam's parents went to Wolbrom because they had no other place to go and because they sought a family network to rely on. Another survival strategy was to create the appearance of normal life. Thus, Sam, together with other Jewish children, attended clandestine classes to continue their education and have a semblance of childhood.

Efforts to create a simulacrum of life before the war while living in the ghettos crumbled when the German regime unleashed dragnet operations against Jews. German forces, with the assistance of the Polish Blue Police, liquidated the ghetto in Wolbrom in September 1942.[7] Some Jews, aware of what awaited them, decided to hide, among them Sam, his mother, his aunts and a cousin. They evaded the collection of Jews in the market square, the selection of the weak and the elderly for murder in the nearby forest and the transfer of the remaining Jews to a railroad station. When Sam and his loved ones emerged from their hiding place after this roundup was over, they did not know where they could go. A German law of

---

6 For an overview of how the persecution of Jews unfolded in Wolbrom, see Samuel Fishman, "Wolbrom," in *The United States Holocaust Memorial Museum Encyclopedia of Camps and Ghettos 1933–1945. Volume II Ghettos in German-Occupied Eastern Europe Part A*, edited by Geoffrey P. Megargee and Martin Dean (Bloomington, IN: Indiana University Press, 2012), 595–596.

7 The Polish Blue Police was named after the colour of their uniforms.

INTRODUCTION xxi

October 1941 imposed a death penalty for any Jew outside a ghetto or a camp, as well as for any gentile who helped a Jew. Of the some 7,000 Jews assembled that day, the German authorities deemed approximately 2,500 men fit for work. They deported the remaining Jews to the Bełżec killing centre. Sam managed to cross to the men's group and join his father. Over the next several days, these Jewish men were transferred to labour camps, Plaszow among them.[8]

Construction of the Plaszow labour camp for Jews (also called Julag I, short for its German term — *Judenlager* (Jewish camp) — or Jerozolimska camp, from the name of the street on which it was situated) began in summer 1942.[9] Workers were brought in from the Krakow ghetto, located less than three kilometres from the camp, as well as from other ghettos in the Krakow region. Isolated from the Polish population, the camp was surrounded by barbed wire and policed by German and Ukrainian guards. A hierarchy of prisoners quickly developed. Although most were assigned to the arduous task of building camp structures, others assumed various types of work that allowed them to stay indoors, receive better treatment and get extra food. Connections to privileged prisoners often made a difference in what job a prisoner landed. Sam's cousin was a camp scribe. He was in a position to recommend Sam to his German supervisor. Sam's knowledge of the German language helped him get a better labour assignment in the camp — as a room attendant and an errand boy for a German officer.

Sam and his father took advantage of the well-disposed German officer and managed to obtain a permit from him to return to

---

8 Płaszów is the name of the district in Krakow where the German camp called Plaszow was located. The Germans did not use the Polish diacritics in the spelling of the camp name.
9 For an introduction to the history of the Plaszow camp, see Ryszard Kotarba, *A Historical Guide to the German Camp in Płaszów 1942–1945* (Institute of National Remembrance – Commission of the Prosecution of Crimes against the Polish Nation, 2014).

Wolbrom. In this first, more haphazard, phase of the camp's existence, supervision of prisoners was not as strictly enforced. Perhaps the German officer was promised something in exchange for his consent. Then too, the German officer knew that the two Jews really had little, if any, possibility of surviving on the "Aryan" side. Sam and his father headed to Wolbrom, where they stayed with a Jewish clearing crew. Such groups existed in other former ghettos too, as their task involved sorting through the belongings of the Jews who had been deported. The father and son managed to leave for Krakow just in time, before the final deportation of the remaining Wolbrom Jews. Since information was not readily available, they gathered from the mail they had received in Wolbrom and from rumours that their only option for survival would be, paradoxically, to re-enter Plaszow.

En route to Krakow, Sam and his father, exhausted from walking some thirty kilometres, spotted a barn in what turned out to be a village outside the town of Słomniki. The response to their appearance highlights the different attitudes and behaviours of gentile Poles toward Jews seeking shelter. Some Poles at this time offered ad hoc or more permanent assistance, thereby risking their own and their family's lives, whereas others blackmailed Jews and extorted valuables from them, and still others outright denounced Jews to the Polish police and German authorities. Prospective and active helpers feared the watchful eyes of their neighbours and, as in the case of Sam's aid giver, their own family members. Unable to keep the two Jews for much longer, the young Polish man took them to Krakow and instructed them on their entry procedure — to bribe their way into the ghetto. Both Polish policemen, who guarded the external perimeter of the ghetto, as well as Jewish policemen, who maintained order inside the ghetto, willingly accepted bribes from Jewish smugglers and other Jews who sneaked into and out of the ghetto. Again, a connection to a Jew who held a more privileged position, this time in the ghetto, helped Sam and his father secure employment and food rations, at least for the next few weeks.

Although their trajectories diverged in the first years of the war, by late 1942 both Sam and Johnny had been confined in the Krakow ghetto. Johnny survived two major German *Aktionen*, or round-ups, in the period from May to June and in October 1942. The latter *Aktion* became etched in the memory of ghetto inhabitants, including Johnny's, as the most brutal. Still, he carried on. At first, Johnny worked at Oskar Schindler's Emalia factory, which produced enamelled dishes and bullet shells for the German war effort. Schindler, a German businessman, was focused on maximizing profit through exploiting the forced labour of Jews. At the same time, his awareness of the Jews' situation in the ghetto led him to treat his labourers less harshly than they would have been elsewhere. Therefore, Emalia was a desirable workplace and bribery flourished among those seeking to get an assignment there. That is probably how Johnny lost his assignment there to a replacement worker. In mid-January 1943, Johnny was forced out of the ghetto and into the Plaszow camp. Sam did not stay in the ghetto for much longer either. By mid-March 1943, the German authorities had liquidated the Krakow ghetto. The Germans murdered a number of Jews and shipped the rest to Auschwitz. They transferred those deemed able-bodied, including Sam and his father, to Plaszow.

In January 1944, Plaszow formally became part of the concentration camp system, and the camp commandant had to follow procedures set in Berlin. Plaszow itself was not only a place of exploitative labour, but also a site of killing and a transit camp for Jewish slave labourers. Johnny was transferred to Auschwitz in February 1944. Sam also survived major selections and deportations. But as the Soviet Red Army was making its way from the east, the Nazis in Berlin decided to erase all traces of their atrocities and destroy evidence of the existence of Plaszow. Sometime in the summer or fall of 1944, Sam was shipped to Gross-Rosen concentration camp. The final transport left Plaszow in October, while the last remaining prisoners were marched to Auschwitz on January 14, 1945. Four days later, on January 18, the Red Army arrived in Krakow.

Johnny and Sam's suffering continued as they were shuffled to other camps: Falkenberg and Bergen-Belsen (Sam) and Mauthausen, Melk, Gusen and Gunskirchen (Johnny). They describe how camp life was organized and the daily struggle to survive. Often, forming a network or aligning with another prisoner helped in the unpredictable environment of the camp. In such arrangements, inmates looked out for one another. But, as the histories of both Sam and Johnny show us, luck was ultimately the reason for their survival. We learn, too, about the prisoners' harrowing journeys on death marches from camp to camp with little to no food or water, in inadequate clothing, exposed to the elements, exhausted and sick.[10] The Nazis were determined to exploit the prisoners for slave labour. The inmates could only surmise from the changing behaviour of the German guards and from the transfers from camp to camp that favourable circumstances were no longer on Germany's side.

In spring 1945, Sam and Johnny were liberated.[11] Quite remarkably, both authors devote much attention to how they navigated the new post-war reality. Their recollections illuminate the factors that survivors grappled with in the early post-war period. Chronologically, the Holocaust had ended. But for survivors, their suffering continued. Both Sam and Johnny were homeless, orphaned and helpless. They entered displaced persons (DP) camps: Sam was in Bergen-Belsen in Germany (in the British zone), and Johnny was in Wels, and later Bindermichl, both in Austria (in the American sector). Over a quarter million Jews passed through such camps located in Germany, Austria and Italy. The United Nations Relief and Rehabilitation Administration (UNRRA) administered the DP camps. The American

---

10 For a study on this topic, see Daniel Blatman, *The Death Marches: the Final Phase of Nazi Genocide*, trans. Chaya Galai (New York: Belknap Press, 2013).

11 For a study on the experience of liberation and post-war displacement, see Dan Stone, *The Liberation of the Camps: The End of the Holocaust and Its Aftermath* (New Haven, CT: Yale University Press, 2015).

Jewish Joint Distribution Committee (JDC, the Joint) provided extensive help to Jewish DPs in the form of food, medicine, clothes and equipment, but also resources for cultural, educational and religious endeavours. In the DP camps, survivors recuperated and regained hold of their lives.

Part of that process involved a search for surviving relatives. The Central Committee of Liberated Jews, an organization run by survivors in DP camps, drafted lists of individuals' names and hometowns, and then transmitted them from one DP camp to another. That is how Sam learned about his surviving relatives. Another way to locate family was through the Central Tracing Office (now the International Tracing Service). Johnny reconnected with his uncle in Switzerland through that bureau. Johnny's epistolary interaction with a relative who did not experience the Holocaust, since he had been living in a neutral state already before World War II, highlights some of the reactions to survivors and to their wartime experiences.

Another issue occupied most survivors: emigration. DP camps were temporary places of residence (the last camp, Foehrenwald, closed in 1957). Where could the displaced Jews go? Their native Poland was not an option for Sam or Johnny. Out of Poland's pre-war Jewish population of about 3.3 million, barely 10 per cent survived, most of them having fled deeper into the Soviet Union. While some Jewish survivors were determined to rebuild their lives in Poland, others crossed the border into Germany with the aim to emigrate further and build their lives elsewhere. The lack of surviving relatives, an image of Poland as a site of destruction and fear of antisemitism effectively discouraged many Jewish survivors from settling in Poland. (A pogrom in the city of Kielce in July 1946 in which local Poles killed over forty Jews was a watershed event for survivors that confirmed that they had no future in Poland.) Then too, many Jewish homes had been appropriated by ethnic Poles. Jews, already possessing nothing, had nowhere to go; and they were often not welcome.[12] With Poland falling under the Soviet sphere of influence and the institution of a communist regime in the country, practising Judaism and rekindling Jewish life became difficult.

Unable and unwilling to return to Poland, both Sam and Johnny awaited their turn to immigrate to North America. Eventually, Sam travelled to Canada via the United States, and Johnny went directly to Canada. Palestine was another option for many Jews. Zionist activists in the DP camps advocated for Jews to go there. However, under British rule, Palestine was off limits. In spite of that, over 100,000 Jews attempted to enter Palestine illegally, with the help of Jewish underground movements. When the State of Israel was pronounced in May 1948, thousands of Jews flocked to the nascent Jewish state where they could finally feel at home. But Israel was not an easy place to live. The country experienced an influx of refugees at the time when it was only being developed and endured conflicts with the Arab population. Sam was discouraged from making his way there. He switched his destination to North America, where he already had some familial ties. Johnny, by contrast, ended up in Canada by accident and thanks to a dose of luck — he managed to register as an orphan with the Canadian Jewish Congress, which then brought him to his new home.

Determined to leave the DP camps and resume their lives free of confinement and uncertainty, some survivors adopted creative exit modes, from being smuggled to Palestine to changing their identities. Both Sam and Johnny engaged in the latter, albeit for different reasons. Assuming a different name and providing falsified personal information carried its own set of difficulties that the two did not anticipate. Adopting new identities worked in the short run — both

---

12 Jan Gross, *Fear: Anti-Semitism in Poland After Auschwitz. An Essay in Historical Interpretation* (New York: Random House, 2006).

young men managed to arrive in North America and create new lives there. In the long term, changing their identities made it more difficult for them to be traced by surviving relatives and friends many years after the war. And it diminished, if not inhibited, their chances of restitution of property left in Poland and of receiving compensation from the German government for their wartime persecution. Sam, in particular, highlights these issues in his memoir.

What mattered most to Sam and Johnny was that they could start their lives anew in countries not directly affected by the Holocaust. Their recollections highlight the complex process of adjustment experienced by newcomers and, in the case of both Sam and Johnny, by refugees and survivors of genocide.[13] The help of familial and social networks, as well as of organizations, such as the Canadian Jewish Congress and HIAS (Hebrew Immigrant Aid Society), proved crucial for new immigrants to find housing, training opportunities and jobs, but also to help them resume their education or learn English. Yet, immigrants such as Johnny were eager to break free from organized assistance and live on their own. They believed that the social workers had little understanding of the specific needs of Holocaust survivors and of the individualized approaches their cases demanded. In addition, some local members of the Jewish communities with whom survivors interacted had a skewed image of refugees from Eastern Europe as people who needed to be instructed on table manners or the use of household equipment. The patronizing attitude was demeaning to many survivors.

Issues of perception and adjustment emerge in these two personal recollections, which provide insight into the experience of refugees and newcomers, into their needs and expectations. The memoirs of Sam and Johnny, while focusing on how, with the much-needed

---

13 Adara Goldberg explored the issues of absorption and integration of Holocaust survivors in Canada in *Holocaust Survivors in Canada: Exclusion, Inclusion, Transformation, 1947–1955* (Winnipeg: University of Manitoba Press, 2015).

external help, they managed to build fulfilling lives after the trauma they had suffered, do not shy away from elaborating on the less positive aspects of that process. Such straightforward accounts could emerge only after a passage of time. The authors challenge the common misconception that after being liberated survivors reestablished their lives quickly and smoothly. This part of survivors' post-war lives is often not understood sufficiently, and Holocaust scholarship has yet to address this topic in a comprehensive way.

Sam's and Johnny's memoirs are multilayered, individual histories. They offer a glimpse into the lives of young Jewish Poles in the interwar period. They open a window onto the decisions, actions and events that shaped how each of the two men experienced the war and the Holocaust. In doing so, these two memoirs provide a more refined understanding of how the Holocaust progressed on a local level. However, the two accounts render more than a historical perspective. From a psychological angle, they explore human behaviour in extreme situations and highlight various coping mechanisms. These personal narratives speak of unimaginable loss and destruction. But they also illuminate moments of humanity even in the darkest of times. When the war ended, survivors strove to reestablish their lives. These two candid accounts of that process elucidate the survivors' hopes, hurdles and accomplishments. The titles of Sam's and Johnny's memoirs implore readers to remember and to share their histories both as a warning of what could happen when ideology and hate prevail and as a way to commemorate those who did not live to tell their own stories.

Joanna Sliwa
The Conference on Jewish Material Claims Against Germany (Claims Conference)
2018

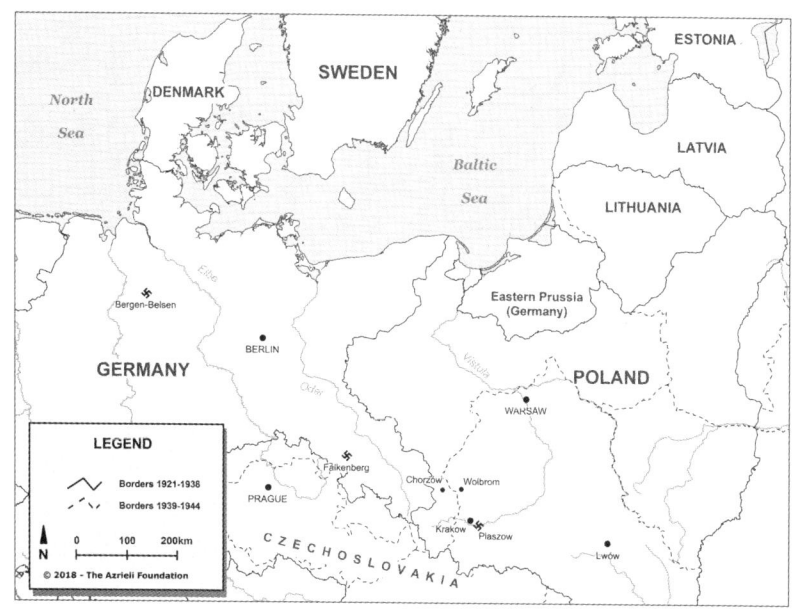

MAP FOR SAM WEISBERG

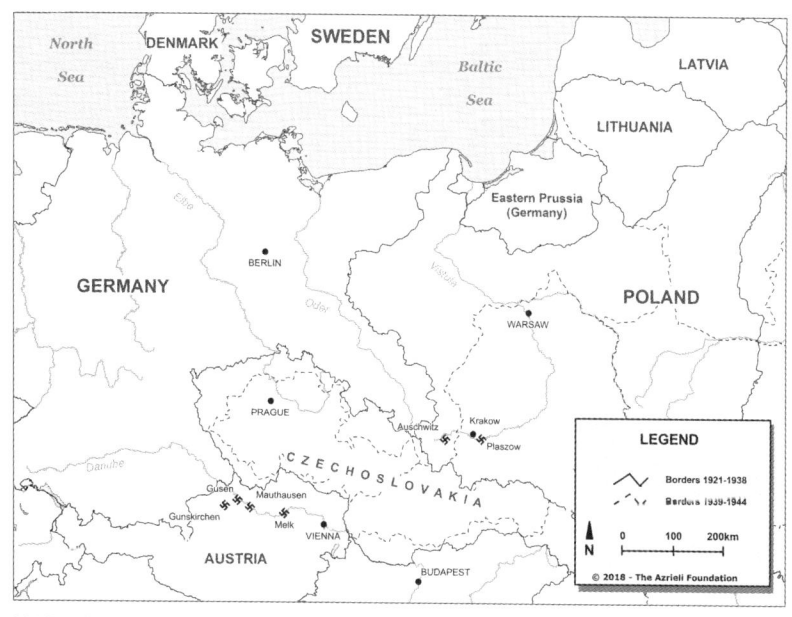

MAP FOR JOHNNY JABLON

CARRY THE TORCH
Sam Weisberg

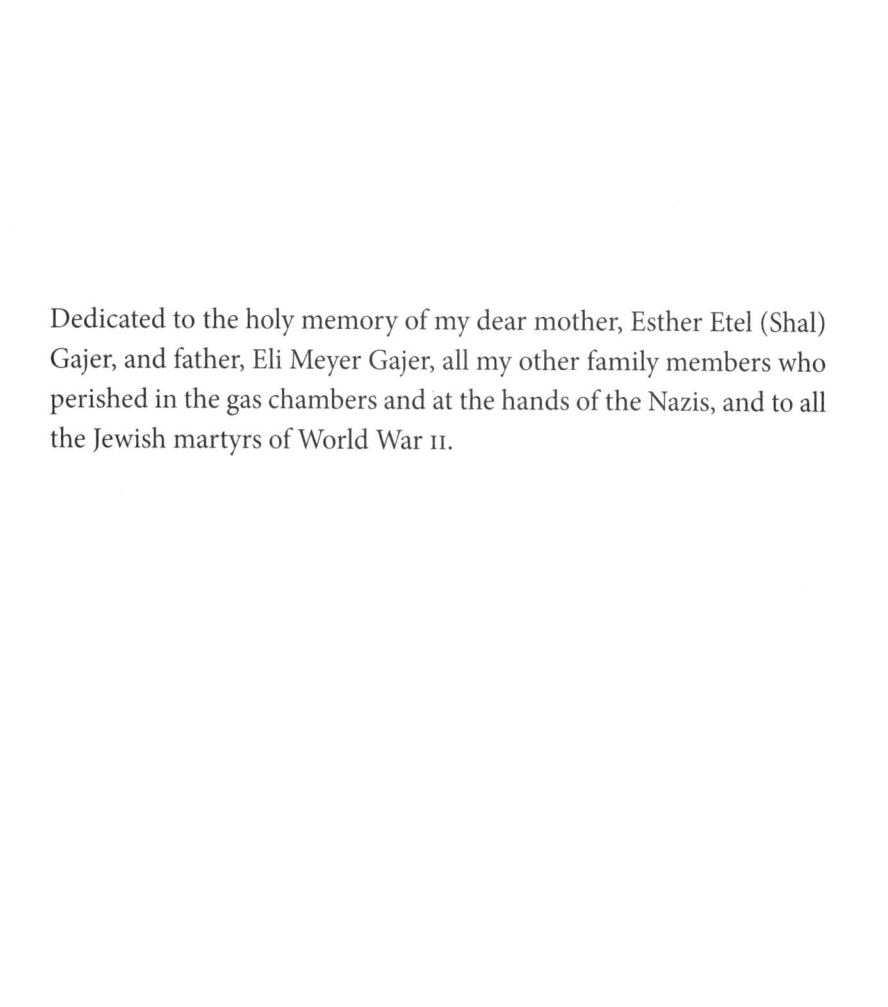

Dedicated to the holy memory of my dear mother, Esther Etel (Shal) Gajer, and father, Eli Meyer Gajer, all my other family members who perished in the gas chambers and at the hands of the Nazis, and to all the Jewish martyrs of World War II.

Polish Roots

My father, Eli Meyer Gajer, was born in Lutowiska, a small town in Galicia, Poland. He was one of six siblings and had three brothers, David, Anshel and Akiva, and two sisters, Chaya and Faige.

My mother, Esther Etel Shal, was born in Niemirów, also in Galicia. She was the oldest of four sisters, the others being Shaiva, Bela and Raisel. My mother came from a very religious home, and her grandfather (or perhaps her great-grandfather) was the rabbi of Lubaczów, a town near Niemirów. When she got married, she kept a very kosher home as well.

My parents met and got married in Krakow, Poland, in the early 1920s. My father had gone there to find work since there was little to do in his hometown, and my mother went there with her sisters because there was more opportunity in the big city.

My mother was an ardent Zionist, and soon after they got married, my parents fulfilled their lifelong dream of going to Israel (British Mandate Palestine at the time). I don't know anything about their illegal journey or how they got there, but once they were settled, they became the proud owners of a small ice cream shop in Jerusalem called HaSharon Café.

Unfortunately, despite my parents' hard work and determination, their dream was short-lived, and they only stayed in Palestine for about two years. My father's stomach was constantly upset, and it became increasingly obvious that he had a digestive problem. Several doctors suggested that the difference in the climate between Europe and Palestine, particularly the extreme heat, was the cause. My parents concluded that they had to leave for my father's health.

After returning to Krakow, my mother and her three sisters opened a wig shop. The sisters worked as a team to make the shop a success, but they especially relied on Shaiva, who as a young woman had apprenticed as a wig maker in their hometown. Weaving each individual lock of hair by hand, they created custom-made *sheitls*, wigs, for religious Jewish women.

In the mid-1920s, within a few years of opening the shop, each sister married in succession. My aunt Shaiva married Yechiel Brühand. He was a very successful engineer, although he probably did not have a formal degree, since it was very hard for Jews to get university degrees in those days. He built his own buildings, a few of which are still standing in Krakow. One of them is at 14 Warszawska Street.

Bela married Moshe Spiegler, and Raisel, the youngest of the sisters, who had a stutter, married a very religious person. They had a daughter together, Ada, but after only a year, he left Raisel and their baby.

In 1925, my mother gave birth to a son, Moshe. Unfortunately, he passed away when he was only six weeks old, probably from what we now call crib death or sudden infant death syndrome. In 1926, my parents moved to Chorzów, a city in the southern district of Silesia, Poland. Chorzów was originally in Germany, where it was called Königshütte, but in 1918, when many European borders were redrawn as a result of World War I, the city fell into Polish hands and was then known as Królewska Huta for a while. When my parents moved there, the population was still about 40 per cent German. Chorzów was a border town near Bytom, Germany, but the border itself was only a formality. The two cities were only eight kilometres apart and were connected by a streetcar that, in the early 1930s, ran every half hour.

On October 22, 1927, I arrived on the scene and my parents called me Avraham Ichak Gajer. When I was born, we were living in an apartment in a complex on Trzeciego Maja Street (Third of May Street), named to celebrate the declaration on May 3, 1791, of the constitution of the Polish–Lithuanian Commonwealth. Gurecky, the owner of the complex, operated a drugstore on the ground floor, and we had a two-room apartment on the second floor. There was a kitchen with a stove and a dining area in the first room, and the second room was used as a bedroom and for storage. A curtain functioned as a divider between the two rooms.

Chorzów was an industrial city that had a steel foundry and was surrounded by coal mines, so the air quality was poor due to fumes and dust. At the age of four, I developed whooping cough and then later wound up with bronchial asthma, from which I still suffer today. My mother became my nurse. She was very careful with me, but the asthma got so bad that, on the countless nights when I had an attack, my poor mother had to carry me in her arms until I finally fell asleep. She believed the asthma was a consequence of the whooping cough, but I think it was likely due to the industrial pollution.

When they moved to Chorzów, my parents opened a small ready-to-wear men's and boy's clothing store on Trzeciego Maja Street. Both my parents worked in the store, and my mother even designed some of the clothes they sold. My father was very energetic and a very good businessman. He would give his ready-to-wear clothes to self-employed salespeople on consignment and they, in turn, would sell the clothes door to door.

Many Germans were in need of ready-to-wear clothing and used to cross the border on the streetcar to shop at our store. They would arrive with torn clothes, buy new things to wear from my parents and dump their old clothes before they left. The number of Germans crossing the border to shop at our store increased even more a few years later when Adolf Hitler was elected chancellor of Germany; Hitler was preparing his army for war and diverted much of Germany's money to armaments, increasing Germans' need for foreign-made clothing.

Because the clothes were so affordable, the business was a huge success. My father, who was not very religious, kept the store open on Saturdays, but he did close it on Jewish holidays, like Rosh Hashanah and Yom Kippur. The store had become so well known all around Silesia that, around 1930 or 1931, my parents moved the shop to a much larger space about four or five blocks away at the corner of Koscielna Street (Church Street) and Trzeciego Maja Street, where our apartment was. The new shop had two entrances, one on each street, and four large display windows that faced both streets, something that was unusual for that time. My parents employed a full staff of salespeople and hired my mother's cousin Meyer to do the bookkeeping and accounting. He was a very learned person and a great help in the business.

Around that same time, when I was around four or five years old, my parents decided to move us into more comfortable living quarters. The new apartment was on Koscielna Street, right across the street from the store, and I have vivid memories of that apartment. It was much larger and more modern than our old apartment, with three bedrooms, a kitchen and a bathroom equipped with a gas-fired water heater and a bathtub.

When I was around six years old, my brother Yehezkel Yosef was born. He was a beautiful blond child, pleasant and quiet.

My mother was very busy, since she was involved in the business and taking care of a new baby. I was becoming a bit of a problem as I grew, running through the long corridor in the apartment and always wanting to go out to play with other kids, so my mother hired a nanny to keep track of me and watch the baby. She also hired a young Polish woman named Yanina to look after the housekeeping. The nanny, Greta, was of German descent and spoke to us in German; I became more fluent in German than in Polish. When I later started school, I had difficulties because I didn't speak Polish very well. I had to learn the official language of the country where I was born in a classroom.

In the summer of 1934, just before I turned seven and was about to enter school, my father decided that he wanted to show me off to his parents, Hersh Leib and Lika Gajer. They still lived in Lutowiska, Galicia, south of Lwów, where my father was born. My father and I travelled by train for several hours to get there and had to complete the final leg of our journey riding for an hour in a horse-drawn buggy.

Lutowiska was a very small town, almost a village, which consisted of a square and a smattering of farms. There was a population of several hundred people, and very few of them were Jews. My grandparents had a tiny store in the front room of their very small house, which only had three or four rooms, including the store. They sold grains, such as corn and wheat, which they stored in large sacks. There was a large scale hanging by a chain from the ceiling, and people would come to buy a kilo of this or a kilo of that.

My grandfather was Hasidic-looking and wore a *kapote*, a long black coat, and a *kippah*, a religious skullcap, and my grandmother was very caring. They were both very kind to me, but try as they might, I wouldn't stop crying. Being so young, I was distressed to be separated from my mother. The only thing that helped was when my grandfather took me across the street to see the neighbour's ponies — I even got a pony ride around the village.

My relatives spoiled me when I was there and tried everything possible to keep me happy. Aunt Faige, my father's sister, and her husband owned a small tavern with a guest house overlooking the town square on the main street. Their establishment was perhaps too tiny to really be considered a tavern, but it was the main source of entertainment for the villagers and the surrounding farmers, who came there to play pool or have a drink of ale. I was very impressed that the tavern had a billiard table. Faige and her husband even let me play billiards to try to make me happy, but nothing stopped me from whining and crying that I wanted to go home.

On our way home, we stopped for a few days to visit my uncle

Akiva Gajer, who lived in a small village a little over an hour from Lutowiska. What struck me most about him was his large stature. He had a wife and two children, whose names I do not remember, and owned a sawmill that consisted only of a large saw mounted on a table. The villagers used to bring whole tree trunks with the branches removed and run them through the big blade on the table. This produced long, rough-looking boards, which I suppose they used for building.

When we left, my father told me that I had another uncle, Anshel, who lived in Drohobych, which was considered an important city because of its oil reserves. Later, I found out I also had another aunt, Chaya, who lived with her family in the district of Polesie, a little north of Galicia. Unfortunately, I never met any of these relatives. I never saw my grandparents or my aunt and uncle again either; I heard that they were all killed by their neighbours during the war so that they could get possession of my family's house and tavern.

I also took a trip with my mother that summer to her hometown, Niemirów. She wanted to show me off to her family too. We stayed with Mother's very tall cousin, Yosele, and his family, including a little girl about my age. There was no electricity in Niemirów, a small village close to Rava-Ruska, so oil lamps and candles were used for light. I was used to refrigerators at home, but here houses had a trap door in the floor with a ladder down to the basement, where the dairy products were kept.

One night, I awoke to a lot of commotion and bells pealing on the street. I went outside and Yosele and the others were watching a barrel-like horse-drawn carriage steered by two helmeted men go by. It was the fire brigade on its way to put out a fire. Like my family on my father's side, all of my family in Niemirów also perished in the Holocaust.

When we got back to Chorzów, I started school. My parents sent me to a non-religious Jewish school, where we studied Polish, geography, mathematics and literature. The school was located on Kasimir

Street, named for Kasimir the Great, the king of Poland from 1333 to 1370, who consorted with a Jewish woman, Esterka, and was responsible for establishing and protecting the Jewish district in Krakow. The school's surrounding neighbourhood had a large Jewish population and strong Jewish character. There were two kosher restaurants and a kosher butcher on the same block.

On the ground floor of our school building there was a *shtiebl*, a small Orthodox synagogue, and a kosher poultry slaughterhouse. In our school, all the students and teachers were Jewish, and our classrooms were located on the second, third and fourth floors. Across the street from the school stood a somewhat conservative synagogue, an impressive building in the style of German temples and synagogues. In this synagogue, women sat in balconies separate from the men and there was a choir that performed on the third floor. The *bima*, the main podium, was unusual in that it was like a stage at the front of the synagogue. The rabbi and cantor wore fine *kittels*, white robes, and, sometimes, they even wore top hats. The whole synagogue and the way the people there looked and acted were impressive to me. Unfortunately, I only got to attend services there on Yom Tov, the High Holidays, and other special occasions.

In the same building where I attended day school, Hebrew classes were taught in the afternoons after regular classes. Because of my health issues, my mother felt I wasn't strong enough to attend those classes. But since a Hebrew education was very important to her, she had the Hebrew teacher, Mr. Kokoczinsky, come to my home twice a week to teach me privately. My mother staunchly believed that one day Palestine would become a home for the Jewish people and that I would need to know Hebrew to communicate there. Although I did learn some Chumash (Torah), Gemara (Talmud) and prayers, the focus of my Hebrew lessons was conversational, not religious.

My friends in school included Ernst Weistrich, who lived about a block from our house, Lemek Chapnick and a young fellow named Bogomolny. I was also friends with Rutka Erenwort and Lilka Bornstein, the prettiest girls in the class. All of these children were about my age and were in school with me, but none of them survived the Holocaust.

Prosperous and busy, with two little boys at home, my parents had overcome the disappointment of having to leave Palestine and the tragedy of losing their first-born, Moshe. They were starting to enjoy their lives when tragedy struck again.

I remember the day in 1936 when our housekeeper, Yanina, told my mother that Yehezkel had a fever and would not eat. Due to the risk of contagion, I was sent to stay with Aunt Bela and Uncle Moshe Spiegler in Katowice until Yehezkel was better. My father had helped Uncle Moshe open a small ready-to-wear men's clothing store in Katowice similar to my parents' shop, and they lived in an apartment above the shop.

Weeks went by and my parents were so preoccupied with Yehezkel's illness that they were unable to come see me, even though Katowice was only about six kilometres from Chorzów and a thirty-minute trip by streetcar. At that time, Bela and Moshe did not have any children, and I had no company except my uncle and aunt. I missed home terribly and cried all the time. Aunt Bela told me that my little brother had diphtheria, an infection of the throat, and my parents were busy making every possible attempt to cure him.

My parents even brought in a specialist from Vienna to treat him, which in those days was a huge undertaking. When the swelling in his throat began to prevent Yehezkel from breathing, a doctor performed a tracheotomy. A table was set up in the spare room of our family's large apartment and a nurse was brought in. But, despite everything they did, after about six weeks I no longer had a brother.

Even now, so many years later, I cannot imagine how my mother coped with this tragedy. What I do know is that I quickly became the centre of her life. My mother would dedicate every spare moment she had from her work as a wife, homemaker and business owner to me. She called me her *oyg in kop*, the apple of her eye. The expression means she was totally devoted to me. She would take me everywhere with her, including on vacation to resort towns like Krynica, Zakopane and Bystra.

Shortly after I started school in 1934, my nanny Greta got married to a German air force pilot. Since he was from Berlin, she moved there when they married. In 1937 or 1938, she came back to Chorzów to visit her parents and stopped in to see us too. Greta must have had a sense of what was coming, because during that visit she came up with a proposal. She suggested that, due to the increasing tensions between Poland and Germany, she take me to Germany with her, at least for a few months until everything calmed down. But my parents, especially my mother, wouldn't hear of it. Later, however, we realized what a good idea it would have been to take advantage of her proposal.

In the late 1930s, the antisemitic tendencies of the Polish population were becoming more overt, and there were obvious signs of "rot" in the Polish attitudes toward Jewish people. Signs were posted on fences along the street that said, basically, "Away with the Jews but we'll keep the Jewish girls." Jewish children going to and from school were sometimes attacked by non-Jewish kids. There were lots of non-Jews in our area, but the Jews stuck together; we kids did not have much to do with the non-Jewish ones. But the violence became a problem for me and my friends when the non-Jewish boys began to hide in the covered market and hit us as we were passing by. It became so bad that I instituted a form of resistance.

By then I already saw myself as part of the Betar Zionist youth movement and was quite militant. My plan was that one boy would act as a decoy and head out alone past the doorways where the non-Jewish boys lurked, waiting to beat us up with their school bags or fists. When the decoy was attacked, my group of three or four friends would leap out and retaliate. This tactic proved somewhat successful, but our parents believed in pacifism and encouraged us to avoid confrontations by crossing to the other side of the street. Despite the overtness of the hatred and the radio speeches through the 1930s in which Adolf Hitler proclaimed his view of what should be done with the Jews, most Jewish people thought of it as a temporary situation that would resolve itself.

I recall turning to my mother during one of Hitler's tirades and asking her, "Do you see what's happening?"

My mother replied, "Dear son, that is happening over there. They have a dictatorship. In Poland we have a democracy. We have nothing to fear here."

But my mother did not know that in a speech in January 1939 Hitler would announce that he would annihilate all the Jews of Europe and, less than a year after that, on September 1, German soldiers would march into Poland.

In 1937, my parents took me to Krakow to visit my mother's sister, Aunt Shaiva, and her husband, Yechiel Brühand. They also took me to see their new acquisition, a large property on Aleja Słowackiego in a neighbourhood that, even today, is considered fancy. It was the first time I had ever seen a five-storey building with an elevator, and I insisted on riding it up and down repeatedly, captivated by the feeling and wanting to understand how the mechanism worked. I even memorized the name of the manufacturer: Wertheim, probably a German company.

A couple years later, probably in the summer of 1939, we received a letter from the Polish government's taxation office, the Urzad Skarbowy, indicating that we were a security risk because of our wealth. We were too close to the border and, therefore, would have to leave Chorzów. My parents certainly thought that was odd, but they weren't particularly alarmed. My mother's sister Shaiva, as I mentioned, lived in Krakow, so my parents were happy to move there. They arranged to rent an apartment in Krakow on Floriańska Street near St. Florian's Gate, the historical entrance to Krakow, and my aunt and uncle, Bela and Moshe Spiegler, came to look after our business in Chorzów, which we thought would only be temporary.

Before we left Chorzów, we visited the cemetery to say goodbye to my brother Yehezkel. None of us imagined it would be the last time we would see his gravesite.

Crossing Borders

In late summer of 1939, my mother, my aunt Shaiva, my cousin Ada and I went to Krynica, an exclusive resort known for its healing spring waters and mud baths, *kąpiel borowinowa*, and stayed in a kosher hotel called the Three Roses. Coming from a religious family, my mother took the opportunity to introduce me to Jewish customs, such as the mikvah, the ritual baths, and I went there with one of the other hotel guests. Since I was not used to bathing in public, I did not especially enjoy the steam bath, but I remember the experience well.

Toward the end of our vacation, the hotel porter came looking for my mother or my aunt to answer a telephone call from Krakow. My mother took the call and told me afterward that my father and uncle wanted us to return to Krakow immediately because there were rumours of an impending war.

We returned home to our apartment on Floriańska Street on the first available train. A day or two later, when we were barely unpacked, the first bombs fell on Krakow. Everyone in the three-storey building thought the basement would be the safest place to go when the bombs fell, so that's where we went. It was the first time I had seen the basement.

Meanwhile, back in Chorzów, Moshe Spiegler was called up to military duty and was told to report to his hometown, Wolbrom, about forty-five kilometres north of us. When he left, my aunt Bela and her two children, Avraham and Chaim, fled from Chorzów to join us in Krakow, leaving our family business behind.

Aunt Bela was extremely worried about her husband. For a large sum of money, my father was able to convince a taxi driver to take him and Aunt Bela to Wolbrom to see if they could find Moshe, but they were not successful since the military would not divulge his whereabouts. When my father and aunt returned that same night, our family decided to leave Krakow in a hurry.

Early the next morning, my parents and I, along with Aunt Bela and her sons, went to the railroad station to board a train, any train, heading east. That direction seemed the only safe one, because the Germans were advancing from the west. By noon, we were heading toward Tarnów, a city in southeastern Poland. But we only got as far as Wieliczka, about fifteen kilometres southeast of Krakow, because the Germans had bombed the railroad tracks, ending our travel by train.

We walked a couple of kilometres and ended up near a village. There my mother, aunt, cousins and I rested by the side of the road while my father continued into the town centre, returning an hour later with good news. He had convinced one of the farmers to sell him a horse and a hay wagon loaded with straw and horse feed. With the few possessions we had with us, we climbed aboard and continued east, only stopping when the horse needed to eat or rest. We were accompanied by a string of other people travelling in the same direction, including members of the Polish military. The presence of the soldiers might be why German planes shot at us with machine guns as we travelled.

On the second day of our journey, my father saw planes circle back after flying over us. He screamed at us to get off the wagon and run into the forest. He unhitched the horse and grabbed Avraham, the elder of Aunt Bela's boys at five or six years old, and I grabbed two-year-old Chaim. We all ran toward the trees a couple of hundred feet away. Chaim was too heavy for me to carry that distance, so I found a ditch that had a concrete drainage pipe, and we hid inside it. When the planes passed and we emerged from our hiding places, there were bullet holes on both sides of our wagon and where the horse would have been. We had survived another day.

We continued on our journey and after several days of hard travel finally arrived at the Polish city of Czortków (now Chortkiv, in Ukraine) where my mother's cousin Chana (née Schecter) Steinberg lived. She was married to the local rabbi, Meyer Steinberg, who was also a major in the army and served as a spiritual advisor for Jewish soldiers in Poland.

The very same evening we arrived, the Polish military sent a truck and two soldiers to evacuate Rabbi Steinberg and his family because he was considered to be of military importance. Meyer and Chana packed a few of their belongings and begged us to join them in the truck. The Romanian border was only a few kilometres away and an arrangement had been made to allow this truck to pass through and escape the Germans. Unfortunately, my mother and Aunt Bela would not go along with this proposition. Aunt Shaiva and Uncle Yechiel were still in Krakow and, more distressingly, the whereabouts of Moshe Spiegler was still unknown. My parents and Aunt Bela were still under the impression that things would normalize shortly and we would all be together again. So the Steinbergs and their daughter Duszia continued on to Romania without us. They eventually made it to England. Our decision turned out to be another mistake we made in that time of madness.

A few days after the Steinbergs departed, the Soviets marched in and occupied the eastern part of Poland, including Czortków. By agreement between Hitler and Stalin, Poland was split in two — half for Germany and half for the Soviet Union. Our family, now consisting of me, my parents, Aunt Bela and her sons, decided to move north to Lwów.

In Lwów, my parents and I moved into a small, second-storey apartment consisting of two rooms and a kitchen in a neighbourhood called Łyczaków in the northern part of the city. A short time after we arrived, Uncle Moshe came to join his wife and sons; on account of the occupation, he had been released from the Polish army without ever seeing combat.

Despite all the upheaval, life soon settled back into a sort of routine and my father provided our family with the bare necessities like groceries and rent money by trading on the *birzha*, the underground currency exchange.

I was enrolled at a downtown public school known as the No. 88 Jewish School, twenty minutes from our home by streetcar. Instruction at the school was primarily in Yiddish, which I had just started to learn in Grade 4 in Chorzów. The curriculum also required knowledge of Ukrainian, since Lwów was considered part of Greater Ukraine, and because of the Soviet occupation, we had to learn Russian as well.

Along with the Russian language, we also absorbed Stalin's Soviet political agenda and propaganda at school. I was brainwashed into believing that socialism was the right way to live, which meant that everyone was equal. No antisemitism or discrimination was acceptable. Students who proved themselves academically capable were designated part of the Young Pioneers, a youth organization similar to the Boy Scouts but with a communist orientation. Within months, I was promoted to Pioneer and given a red tie with a chrome pin. The pin had an insignia with an inscription stating *vsegda gotov!* Always Prepared!

My mother's interpretation of "Always Prepared" was to be ready for the life that you chose. Others, however, thought that it meant you should be prepared to defend your country. All of these new ideas influenced my thinking. I thought I was in the right place and that I believed in the right philosophy of life.

One day, though, the slogan "We are all equal" was put to the test. A school friend and I decided we would go see a movie that was highly recommended by the teachers and by the Pioneer leader. The movie was called something like *Our Unbeatable Red Army against*

Finland's Aggression. We went downtown and stood in the long line at the theatre. As we waited, an elderly couple whom we understood to be Jewish passed us and appeared to be looking for friends in the lineup. The woman was wearing a fur coat and seemed well-to-do. As they passed, two people in front of us swore at them in Russian: "Damned Jews are trying to sneak in front of us!"

That was enough to prompt my friend and me to take action. My friend was a local and better versed in Russian; he told me to stay put while he set things straight. He left and came back with two Soviet undercover agents from the NKVD. I knew they were agents, since even though they wore civilian clothes they were well dressed in elegant boots and fur hats, a rarity at the time. My friend pointed out the people who had made the unkind remarks about the elderly couple, and the NKVD men asked them to step out of the movie lineup and escorted them out of sight.

After another half hour of waiting in the freezing cold, we got into the foyer, and while my friend was getting tickets, I noticed the two undercover agents standing with the bigots in the far corner. They were smoking cigarettes and laughing with each other. At that point, I realized that, yes, we were all equal, but some people were more equal than others.

It was common at the time for Soviets to secretly exchange their old golden rubles for American dollars or British pounds under the table. My father was one of their trusted contacts, and one of his clients was a Jewish *politruk*, a military officer involved in promoting Soviet propaganda. This *politruk* befriended my father and started coming for Friday evening visits to our home.

Through him, my father learned that, in order to be eligible for special privileges like medical care and hard-to-get products, one needed a specific passport, which would act as citizenship papers to show that you were born or had lived in Lwów before the war. Newcomers couldn't obtain this passport unless they were considered important and essential to Lwów and the Soviet army.

To get one, my father would need to secure a high-up position in the workforce or an office job. The *politruk* provided my father with a *komandierovka*, a permit giving him the right to purchase a small factory. The permit he obtained was for the purchase of a fictitious factory that supposedly made plywood and was located on the outskirts of Lwów. My father's factory existed only on paper but it would allow him to get the passport he needed.

Then, during the summer of 1940, the Soviet Union decided that all refugees or people originally from outside the Soviet-occupied zone would have to leave or be resettled deeper into the Soviet Union. Those who registered with the government and those who did not have approved government documents were sent away, to Siberia or other far eastern areas of the Soviet Union. Aunt Bela, Uncle Moshe and their two boys, Chaim and Avraham, were shipped off in cattle cars, journeying for more than a week to Aldan, a town in what was then called Yakut ASSR (Autonomous Soviet Socialist Republic), in Siberia. But when a truck with two soldiers came to pick us up, my father showed them the special passport he had obtained and the soldiers saluted and left. We remained in Lwów.

Naturally, my mother was worried about the well-being of her sister and her sister's family, but she calmed down somewhat after receiving a postcard from them with their new address. She began to focus on other things, like my pending bar mitzvah. Under communism, religious practices were illegal, and therefore any religious function had to be concealed and kept quiet. The nearest synagogue to our home was about two blocks away and, like all of the synagogues, had been shut down. However, the former *gabbai*, assistant to the rabbi in running the services, still lived in a little house in the synagogue courtyard. He had hidden a Sefer Torah there and, on occasion, he would allow a minyan, a quorum of ten men, into his home in order to perform a bar mitzvah.

It was arranged that he would teach me my bar mitzvah portion and the blessings. Then my father organized a minyan and, secretively, we snuck into the former *gabbai*'s home. I recited my *brachot*, blessings, in a rush, the Sefer Torah was rolled up and removed, and we left, one by one, as quickly as possible. That was the extent of my bar mitzvah. I didn't wear a *tallit*, a prayer shawl, or *tefillin*, phylacteries, and didn't own any until after the war.

Shortly after Bela and her family arrived in Siberia, my mother got another letter from Bela telling her that Uncle Moshe had died of a heart attack while standing in line waiting to receive bread for his family. In addition to caring for her own family, my mother now took it upon herself to make packages of non-perishable food wrapped in linen sacks (the kind used in grocery stores for flour or sugar) to mail to her sister in Siberia. There was only one post office that would take packages for delivery to the Soviet Union, and my mother would haul these parcels, sometimes weighing as much as twenty pounds, by foot and streetcar to this post office. Despite the difficulty of the undertaking, she did it often enough that Aunt Bela and her family had a reliable source of food. When my aunt returned after the war, she brought one of those empty sugar bags with her. My wife eventually used it to line my *tallit* bag in commemoration of my mother's *tzedakah*, her charitable kindness.

My mother also wanted to find out if her other two sisters and their families were still in Krakow and began to search for them. No mail could pass between the Soviet-occupied part of Poland and the German-occupied part, so she decided that, if she could cross the border, she would make the trip herself and find out what had happened to her family members. My mother packed up a small bag, and then all of us — my mother, my father and I — set out on our journey back to Krakow.

We intended to cross the border near Rava-Ruska (a city now part of Ukraine), only a few kilometres from my mother's hometown of Niemirów, Poland. She still knew a few of the locals in the area and was able to find someone who helped smuggle people across the border at a small creek in a field.

We crossed the creek with a group of others, but there were people waiting for us on the other side: one German soldier, four or five Polish police officers and some local farmers. Maybe our smuggler had tipped them off, because it seemed they had been expecting us. The police officers asked where we were going, and my mother said we were headed back home to Krakow. The other individuals who crossed with us had other excuses, and it seemed they were all good enough that we would be allowed to pass without a problem. One of the farmers pointed at me in my fur-collared coat and said, "How come he has such a good coat? My son could use it." The Polish police officer and the German soldier talked quietly to each other, and then the German soldier demanded that I remove my coat. The Polish farmer grabbed it and ran.

From then on, it seemed we were more or less safe. Our small group of travellers managed to hire a horse and wagon to take us to the town of Zamość, where the nearest railroad station was. The plan was to take the train to Lublin and then get a connecting train to Krakow. Once we got to Zamość, we were told by some local Jewish people that we had better wear armbands with the Magen David, Star of David, on them. If we were caught without armbands, they warned, we would be arrested. So we dutifully wore the armbands when we boarded the train to Lublin.

When we got to the Lublin station, we went toward the ticket booth to get transfers to Krakow and noticed a group of fifteen to twenty people like us, all wearing armbands, standing against the wall of the building as if lined up to buy something. Two German soldiers saw us walking and pushed our little group over to join them. After we had been standing there for a few minutes, two other German soldiers suddenly appeared from an entrance to the lower level. They were wearing white lab coats like doctors wear, but they were splattered with blood.

The "doctors" selected a few people from the lineup and took them down to the basement. My mother panicked, terrified that the Germans were killing people down there. But she felt there was no way out since the two guards were watching over our group to prevent any escape. Twice more the Germans in their blood-splattered coats appeared from the basement, selected four to six people and took them downstairs. Finally, the two Germans returned from the basement without their bloodied coats and spoke with the two guards, who then dismissed the remaining people in the queue, including us.

The incident was terrifying, but that night when we were staying in the Jewish quarter, we learned what it had all been about. The Germans required manual labourers to pluck chickens and found it expedient to use Jews. The episode in the train station and other stories shared by the locals of Lublin scared my parents sufficiently that they decided we should return to the safety of Lwów. My mother wanted to go back the same way we had come, but she didn't want to risk taking the train again, fearful of what might happen when people saw the armbands we now wore. There was an unofficial transportation system of horses and buggies that Jews used to get from place to place, and using this network my mother managed to get us a ride back to Zamość and toward the border.

The horse and buggy was much slower than the train, so we travelled a whole day. Toward evening, as we were passing a small village, the driver told us to crouch down because he saw something that frightened him. As we came closer, we saw there was a smoking building and we could hear people screaming. We later found out that this had been the local synagogue and the screaming people were probably Jews trapped inside.

This time, knowing the procedure, we crossed the border without the interference of the double-crossing locals and eventually made it back to Lwów and our apartment.

To the Other Side

On June 22, 1941, shortly after we returned home, Germany declared war on the Soviet Union, ending their non-aggression pact that they had agreed to less than two years earlier. The Germans marched eastward, pushing through the Ukraine and into the Soviet Union. It only took about a week for the Germans to chase the Soviets out of Lwów, which then became part of German-occupied Poland. Ever efficient, the Germans enacted several new regulations that were similar to those we had experienced in Lublin. Jews had to wear armbands and were restricted in where they could live. They were now to be concentrated in the downtown core, a historically Jewish neighbourhood where the Jewish market used to be.

We didn't live in that area, and when the regulations came into effect our Ukrainian landlord informed us that we would have to move. My parents went down to the Jewish area and found a dingy little room in the back of an apartment building on the main street, Słoneczna Street, Sun Street. We had to leave most of our furniture behind in the old apartment and arrived to find only a couple of beds in the new place but not much else.

A rumour began to circulate that a ghetto would soon be formed, an enclosure in which Słoneczna Street would be included. Now that the Germans had occupied Lwów, there was no longer a border between us and Krakow, so my mother thought she could finally find a way to get us back there. She hoped we would find better housing there and could reunite with our family. She found a German truck driver with a route between Lwów and Krakow who was willing to take us for a substantial amount of money. My parents still had a few things they were able to sell so they could pay him.

We had been living in Lwów for about eight or ten months when a truck pulled up one evening and we hopped into the back with two small suitcases and a pillow for me. There was a German checkpoint just before Krakow, and because it would have been a problem for the truck driver if he were caught bringing Jews into the city, Mother arranged to have our family dropped off at a very small town called Wieliczka, where her cousin's son Meyer Schecter lived, less than twenty kilometres from Krakow. We arrived in Wieliczka at about four in the morning and knocked on Meyer's door. He was extremely happy to see us and welcomed us in.

A day or two later, we learned that some of our other relatives (Aunt Shaiva, her husband, Yechiel, Aunt Raisel and her daughter Ada) had taken refuge in Wolbrom, Uncle Moshe's hometown to the north where Aunt Bela's brother-in-law and sister-in-law also lived. They had left Krakow because food had become scarce and because of the restrictions put on Jewish people there. Since Aunt Bela's brother-in-law Paluch was the local Jewish baker in Wolbrom and because of our family's close relationship, my parents thought that we could at least count on having bread if we went to Wolbrom. So we changed our plans and arranged for a horse and buggy to take us to Wolbrom. It was another full day's trip. When we arrived in Wolbrom, we were reunited with my mother's two sisters, my cousin Ada and my uncle Yechiel. For a short time, anyway, it seemed we had done the right thing.

We got into a daily routine, even though our life was anything but normal. My parents did not work and there was little for me to do. There was no school, no place to play and no entertainment, so we kids were at home all the time. Through my cousin Ada, who was six months younger than me, I met a few other kids our age, and occasionally we would get together at one of their homes to talk about the kinds of things kids talk about.

I was fourteen years old by the time we were living in Wolbrom, and about a month after we arrived, my mother began to ask people she met what would be important for me to know if we won the war. If we didn't win, of course, then nothing would be important. But my parents were still hopeful that things would turn around.

Together with three other families, my mother arranged for a former professor at the Hebrew *gymnasium*, or high school, in Krakow to teach us five teenagers for three to four hours a day. Since the professor had no other income and was displaced like us, this was an attractive opportunity for him, even though it was a dangerous undertaking. Schooling Jewish children was forbidden by the Germans.

We gathered every morning in the attic of a shoemaker's shop and were taught almost one-on-one in this "classroom" — just two benches and a long table. Our lessons included English, mathematics and geography. It was my mother's belief that, if the world ever returned to normalcy, English would be an important language to know. Certainly, learning to speak English helped me immensely after the war.

The danger was that members of the Jewish police and the Polish police would come into the shop periodically for shoe repairs. It would have been disastrous for everyone if the school were discovered, so the shoemaker devised a signal system. When the police were coming, he would take his shoe hammer and hit it three times in quick succession on a metal anvil. With this warning we would go into "silent mode." When it was safe to talk again, he would strike the anvil once and we could resume our class. Attending this school meant we had a new activity to occupy our time. When we weren't in class, we would study together, going over what we had learned at our lessons and preparing for the next ones.

Our lessons continued until September 4, 1942, when the Germans ordered all the Jews in Wolbrom to assemble the following morning at the railroad station. Our family was very scared and perturbed. It was understandable that men could be selected for work details, but it was unclear why everyone, including women and children and older people, had to go. My mother and her sisters decided that their husbands would go to the railroad station but that they, as well as Ada and I, would hide in the attic of Aunt Shaiva's two-storey apartment building. The owners of the building were an elderly couple who did not want to go to the railroad station either and said they would hide with us.

The attic was only accessible from the outside rooftop so, the night before the morning assembly, we said goodbye to my father and uncle. My mother, my two aunts, my cousin Ada, the building owners and I then climbed, one at a time, up a steep ladder onto the roof and through the door into the attic. Once we were all in, Uncle Yechiel and my father removed the ladder.

We waited in that attic for a long time, wondering if anyone would ever return to let us out. Around noon the next day, we heard some noises in the courtyard of the building. Someone identifying himself as Geller, the Jewish police chief, called out our family name, "Gajer," and then he yelled "Etel," my mother's name. Geller had been born in Wolbrom but had lived his whole life in Chorzów and had even written articles in Chorzów's Jewish socialist paper. By trade he had been a painter but had had a hard time eking out a living, so he had occasionally come to my father for financial assistance. Because of this, he felt obligated now to help us. Geller called out again, "Gajer! Open up! Meyer sent me to pick you up." Eventually, my mother relented and opened the hatch, because she knew Geller and believed that my father had sent him.

He told us that because of his position as the Jewish police chief, he had been casually patrolling the station to maintain order when he saw my father at the railroad station and asked him where his wife and son were. When my father told him we were hiding, Geller told my father of the danger if we were found and offered to rescue us from our hiding place. According to Geller's information, all the Jews were being deported and no Jews could remain in Wolbrom. If any were found, they would be shot on sight. My father told him where we were, and Geller then made an arrangement with one of the SS officers at the station. On the condition that we would be brought to the station unharmed, an SS soldier would accompany him the couple of kilometres to our hiding place and we would be brought to the railway station.

Geller and the soldier set the ladder against the building so we could climb down into the courtyard and we were marched in sets of two to the station, with Geller leading us and the SS soldier walking behind us. When we had walked for about a kilometre, it became apparent that the frail older couple were having difficulties keeping up and started trailing farther and farther behind, despite the soldier's cries of "Los, los!" (Get going!) I occasionally looked back and saw the old man stumbling, but my mother told me to keep looking straight ahead. A few minutes later, we heard two shots. The frail old couple had been killed because they could not keep up.

When we got to the railroad station, we were relieved to be reunited with my father and Uncle Yechiel. This relief did not last long, however, as the SS soon gave orders to segregate the men from the women, children and older people. The men were made to stand close to the railroad tracks while the women, children and elderly stood closer to the station.

At one point, my mother realized that those men who were less fit were being taken from the men's side and put into our group, and she concluded that we were on the "wrong" side. Without consulting anyone, she left the queue we were standing in and approached a passing SS soldier. Pointing to me, she told him in perfect German, "This fellow over here came across from the other side."

This was a very risky thing to do. We never addressed Germans directly without first being spoken to. But my mother assumed, because of her perfect German, that she could get away with it, and she did. The SS soldier, with a whip in his hand, immediately started screaming at me, "Geh nach da drüben!" (Get over there!) As he whipped me, I ran over to my father and uncle.

It must have broken my mother's heart to see me whipped. I can only imagine how she must have felt causing me pain in order to save me. But her instincts told her that the side she had sent me to, with my father and uncle, was the side destined for a better outcome. Being only a teenager, I was not as intuitive as my mother. I didn't want to be separated from her, and I was confused by her actions and what I saw as the needless pain they caused me. But I would come to realize that her selflessness and sacrifice saved my life.

That was the last time I saw my mother, Aunt Shaiva and my cousin Ada. They, along with most of the Jews of Wolbrom, were deported to the Bełżec death camp that day, a camp where most who were sent there were killed. My mother was only forty or forty-one years old when she was sent to her death.

The Start of Terror

The able-bodied men, including my father and me, were ordered onto cattle cars and taken by train to the Krakow-Plaszow *Zwangsarbeitslager,* forced labour camp, in a suburb of Krakow. When we got there, we were ordered off the cattle cars at a place generally used for loading livestock and cargo, and marched a few hundred yards to a fenced-in area, known as Julag I, which stood for *Judenlager* I, Jews' camp 1.

We were divided into groups and assigned to barracks. In the evening, we found out that there were only about 250 men at our camp, who were being used to build Julag II (Jews' camp 2). Julag I was located on one side of the railroad tracks and Julag II would be on the other, about half a kilometre away. The tracks ran parallel to the Jerozolimska road, which was the main thoroughfare between Krakow and Wieliczka. Upon completion, Julag II would become the main camp; Julag I would then be dismantled. Julag II in the Plaszow concentration camp is depicted in the movie *Schindler's List.*

The night we arrived, Uncle Yechiel came to the building that Father and I were in and told us that his youngest brother, Benny Brühand, had a position of importance in the camp. Benny had a college education and was the scribe for the camp who kept records of the inmates and was also in charge of work detail lists for Julag II.

Because of his position, Benny was able to keep my father and my uncle on camp duty within Julag I and away from having to do heavy construction work at Julag II. So, for the first few days, we were able to stay together.

At fourteen, I was probably the youngest person in the group and spent my first days hiding in the barracks or pretending I was sweeping the floor with a broom. Although I was largely left alone by the guards at first, we knew that, sooner or later, I would have to have a job. Benny came up with a splendid idea that was probably the reason I survived. Benny's boss, the boss of Julag I, was *Oberscharführer* Miller, and Benny knew he preferred to speak to people in German rather than in Yiddish. He spoke only minimally to Benny even though he was his scribe, since Benny's German was not fluent. But I spoke fluent German, which gave Benny the idea to introduce me to Miller.

When Benny took me to meet his boss, Miller was impressed that a Jewish boy could speak German so well. He asked if I had come from Germany, and I told him I came from Silesia, Poland. Seeing that I could be useful, he told me to stay in Julag I and look after his living quarters. He wanted me to keep his room clean and tidy and to polish his boots. With my new position, I had the liberty to move freely in the camp and could even get food from the kitchen, which I was sometimes able to share with my father and uncle.

As well as taking care of Miller's room, my duties included attending to the needs of the Ukrainian guards, who were commanded by a man called *Oberwachtmeister* Janic. I learned quickly that Janic was jealous of me. He could not speak German as fluently as I could, and Miller preferred conversing with me over him. So I tried to keep out of his way.

Janic was a sadist, and in the month or two I worked for them, I learned what type of animals Janic and the Ukrainian guards were. If an inmate got too close to the camp fence, the Ukrainian guards posted at the watchtower would shoot them on the assumption that they were trying to escape. I suspect that some of these people were not, in fact, trying to escape but were only on their way to the latrine, a pit with a board across it enclosed by a shack. The psychology, I suppose, was to terrify us to the point that we would never even think of escaping.

Janic seemed to take particular pleasure in this "target practice," even kicking their heads in to make sure they were dead. One of my duties was to polish the Ukrainian soldiers' boots, which were left out on the steps of the barracks for me to attend to. One time, while I was cleaning Janic's boots, I saw they were bloody and had some other debris from a skull on them. Janic admitted to me that he had kicked in the skull of someone who had been shot. To him, our lives had no value.

Between Janic and the Ukrainian guards, I felt surrounded by mad dogs. *Oberscharführer* Miller was the only SS officer with whom I had any reasonable rapport. I was just a *Stubendienst*, houseboy, but he treated me relatively well. He spoke to me and would answer if I had a question. One day, as part of my interpreting duties, I came to relay a message to him from the kitchen. During our conversation, Miller told me that Julag II was ready to house inmates and that Julag I would be shut down.

When I told this to my father, we decided we should find a way to leave and get back to Wolbrom. We still hoped we could learn what had happened to our family and to our residence and my uncle's residence.

Benny had told me that he felt I should have better clothes now that I was working for Miller and Janic, but at that time, my father and I were walking around in the rags we had arrived in. At best we might have had a spare pair of underwear. All our clothes and everything else we had was still in Wolbrom at our old residence at 49 Polna Street. My father and I decided we would try to go back there to get our clothes and belongings.

So I went to Miller and asked him if it was possible to obtain a permit to go retrieve some clothes from Wolbrom, as I had insufficient clothing with me. I also asked him if, since I was so young, my father could accompany me. Miller was receptive and told me to return the next day. The next morning, he hand-wrote a permit allowing us to go to Wolbrom as long as we reported back in ten days.

Because of the permit, we were able to get train tickets for the first part of the trip and had no problem getting onto a train. But we had to hitchhike the rest of the way. We travelled without incident though, and when we arrived in Wolbrom, we discovered that Geller and his Jewish police officers were still in town. A couple of dozen men had also been left behind and were responsible for clearing out belongings from Jewish homes. They were sorting out clothing and possessions and bringing them to storage units near the railway station.

Although our clothes had already been taken away, we found other shoes and clothes that fit us. While in Wolbrom, we were also able to check our mail and found a letter from our cousins in Niemirów. They said that they had seen my mother, Shaiva, Raisel and Ada on a train bound for Bełżec. The letter also said that they had heard Bełżec was a very bad camp and no one ever returned from there.

At first, my father didn't think that these cousins really knew much about what my mother and her family would experience at Bełżec. I had been crying for my mother since she was taken away and didn't know what to think. After the war, the truth about Bełżec came out. It has been proven that this camp was a testing ground for how to kill a lot of people in a very short time using gas chambers. The Nazis used fumes from cars and diesel trucks (carbon monoxide gas), which meant the victims died a horrible death with much suffering, because it could take about twenty-five to thirty minutes for them to choke on the fumes.

We stayed in Wolbrom for about a week, hoping that the Jewish police and remnant workforce would be given permission to stay on and that we could remain with them. But this was not to be. Only one day in advance of the deportation, we found out through Geller that

Wolbrom was to be *Judenfrei*, free of Jews. All remaining Jews would have to report to the railroad station to be shipped to a labour camp.

Father and I told Geller that we still had our pass from Miller and that we were not interested in being sent to an unknown labour camp. But where would we go? He found out from a non-Jew who had recently returned from Krakow that Julag I was no longer in existence. He also told us about a Jewish ghetto near Krakow on the other side of the Vistula River in a district known as Podgórze. Father thought that it was not a good idea to go to an unknown place and said he would rather seek out Miller and see if he could place us in Julag II.

To avoid being deported with the remaining Jews the next day, my father and I hid, without Geller's knowledge, in the attic of an Orthodox *shtiebl*, which was so small we could only lie down. We remained in hiding the whole day of the deportation, and in the dark of early morning the next day, we emerged and began our journey toward Krakow.

We were afraid to go to the railroad station, so we set out on foot through the fields. As evening approached, my father sensed that we would have to rest because of my fatigue. He spotted a farm on the outskirts of Słomniki, a small village south of Wolbrom, that had a large barn where, he thought, we might be able to sleep. We approached it from the side and saw the barn's huge door with a smaller, person-sized door in it. But as we tried to enter, someone shouted, "Halt, or I'll shoot!"

Inside the barn was a young man, about twenty years old. He asked us what we wanted, and my father said, "We are at your mercy. We are Jewish people and we are on our way to Krakow. We need somewhere to sleep for a few hours."

The young man looked at me and said, "Climb the stepladder behind the door and go up into the hay. In the morning you can continue."

My father thanked him profusely. But, as we were getting settled, I could see through the cracks in the boards that the door of the farmhouse had opened and someone else had come out. We overheard an argument between the young man and an older man. I heard the older man say, "I can get a bag of sugar and another bag of flour if I tell the German police that Jews are hidden here." The young man became so furious that he hit the older man, shouting, "No way will you sell people for sugar!"

We found out later that the young man's name was Mr. Wilzek and that the older man was his father. My father was afraid the older man might still turn us in, but it turned out that the younger man was the boss of the household.

After a few hours of sleep, my father shook me awake. Young Wilzek was already in the barn, preparing a horse and a hay wagon. He had decided that we could not walk the distance to Krakow without armbands, but that if we had armbands we would be shot, because the Jews of Słomniki had already been deported to concentration camps. So Wilzek offered to take us to the ghetto outside Krakow. We agreed, climbed into his wagon and covered ourselves in the hay.

Young, courageous Wilzek did as he promised. He was somewhat familiar with the ghetto, and as we approached it, he told my father about the two gates we would have to pass through. The first would be guarded by Polish police, and to get past them Wilzek suggested that my father show them our permit and slip them some money. At the second gate, there would be Jewish police and we could tell them the truth. My father took out money to pay Wilzek for his kindness, but despite our insistence, he refused. "For this I can't take money. Save it; you'll need it," he told us. My father told me later that he took a bundle of money and left it under Wilzek's seat in the wagon anyway.

After we crossed the bridge to Podgórze, my father and I hopped off the wagon and Wilzek watched as we approached the first gate with the Polish police officer. We showed him the permit with the money in it, and as predicted, he took the money and let us pass. The Jewish police had no problem letting two Jews into the ghetto.

We felt more secure in the ghetto than we had in the hay wagon, but now the task was to find *Oberscharführer* Miller. After some investigation, my father learned that with the closure of Julag I, Miller had lost his post. We now had no one to turn to. Our journeys had taken us to Czortków, Lwów, Wolbrom and now back to Krakow.

We knew hardly anyone there, but slowly started to find out some things. The ghetto was run by a committee of Jewish people known as the Judenrat. Our relatives, the Brühands, were not in the Krakow ghetto. We eventually learned that Uncle Yechiel had been sent to Julag II. The same person who told us about Uncle Yechiel had connections with the Judenrat, and thanks to these connections, we were able to obtain a food ration pass and find employment inside the ghetto.

Within the ghetto there were a few factories, which manufactured brooms, brushes, shoes and other items needed for the German military. It was faster and cheaper to ship things to the front from Poland than from Germany, especially with the free labour. One of these factories was the Bürstenfabrik, where various kinds of brushes were made, including scrub brushes, shoe brushes and brushes for polishing. Before the war, the factory had been owned by the Jewish Saltzman brothers, and three of these brothers had stayed on. Two of them were involved in the manufacturing process, while the oldest brother, Srulik, specialized in sorting materials such as horsehair for length and quality. Although the brushes were produced for the Germans, the materials were often confiscated from the Polish people.

This is where my father and I were hired. The work there was generally better and less taxing than the hard work that existed beyond the gates of the ghetto, so we were relieved to have it. For a short while in 1942, we lived and worked in the ghetto. Then the Germans, with the help of the Jewish police, began to forcibly remove people to Auschwitz and other forced labour camps like Plaszow. My father and I were among the first group of workers at the Bürstenfabrik to be sent as a group to Julag II, where we continued to make brushes.

The setup of the brush workshop, the Bürstenbinderei, in Julag II consisted of a large building with benches and tables where the workers sat. My father was one of the people who worked at the benches. Because I was young and agile, one of the Saltzman brothers chose me to be a borer. My job as a borer consisted of drilling precision holes into wooden handles by hand, through which people at the tables would then string the appropriate material, completing the brush. There were only five of us borers supplying handles for the approximately forty people stringing them. This job allowed me to stay with my father.

We were in this situation for about a month. Before we left for work each day, we got black coffee and a slice of bread, which was considered a reasonable amount of food at the time. When we returned at the end of the day, we would get soup and another piece of bread. To get from our sleeping quarters to the manufacturing quarters, we had to pass through a gate where we were counted each time. Every morning, at the general assembly point called the *Appellplatz*, the entire camp was counted — each building was counted separately, in rows of five. This count was in addition to the count at the gate going to and from work.

One morning, a big man showed up at the *Appellplatz*. I had heard about him before but had never seen him. His name was *Hauptsturmführer* Amon Göth. He had a dog with him and he walked around arrogantly, as though we did not exist. The next morning, Göth once again strode around the *Appellplatz*, this time accompanied by *Oberscharführer* Miller, my former boss. Although I thought it would be opportune if Miller recognized me, he did not see me.

The police officer in charge of escorting us to and from our work quarters had known the Brühands in Krakow, and I told him that Miller would be pleased to know that I was there, even though Miller and I had not seen each other since he had given me the pass to go to Wolbrom. A day or two later, I was summoned to the station by the Jewish police chief, Hilowicz. He told me that he had relayed my message and that Miller had said to have "the person" come to meet him that evening at the station. I did not know if Miller even knew whom Hilowicz had meant and was skeptical because Hilowicz spoke German with a strong Yiddish inflection, which I remembered Miller did not like.

That afternoon, after my shift at the factory, I rushed over to the police station, but no one was there. I waited for about an hour and then I heard a dog barking and saw Miller and another man approaching the camp from the villa. They passed through a gate and headed straight to the station. I was very afraid. On the one hand, I wanted Miller to help me. On the other hand, he would ask me where I had been. I was supposed to have just fetched my clothes and returned within ten days, but I had taken off for weeks. But when Miller opened the door to the police station and saw me, he simply said, "Oh, it's you!"

I replied, "Ja!" (Yes!) I was about to try to explain that we had been held up by the local authorities, but he said, "Forget it. I want to introduce you to your new boss." He had me come outside where the other man was waiting. While I stood at attention, Miller introduced me to Amon Göth as his previous houseboy and said that I was *leidlich gut*, reasonably good. He suggested that if Göth needed a houseboy, I was a good candidate.

Göth looked at me and said, "Come in the morning."

I was numb for a moment, but then I found my voice. I stood up straight like a soldier and informed him that I was a borer in the factory and was required to report in the morning to work unless I had permission. Göth smiled and said he would take care of it.

Sure enough, that night Hilowicz came running to the sleeping quarters. He said I did not have to go to work in the morning but should report to the villa instead and pick up a special armband that was being sewn for me by the women in the tailoring division. It read, "Bote Bürstenfabrik" (brush factory messenger) and allowed me to move freely through the camp and even pass through the gate to the villa. Once through that gate, I could have even continued on to the main road, Jerozolimska, and beyond to Krakow. But I assume that, knowing I was only fifteen years old and had a father in the camp, Göth felt I would not escape. Where would I go?

Amon Göth appears in the movie *Schindler's List*, in which he is shown shooting prisoners from his villa balcony as target practice. I was, unknowingly, also portrayed in the movie. Imagine my surprise when I saw "myself" onscreen. There is a scene showing me walking toward the gate while Göth is shooting at people.

One of my duties in my new job was to look after Göth's two infamous dogs. They were very well-trained police dogs, and Göth had only to point his finger and the dogs would know to chase and corner someone, even at a significant distance. When the person was cornered, Göth would shoot. I saw this happen at least half a dozen times. Göth took pleasure in this moving target practice.

The dogs were actually very friendly to me. I looked after them, brushing them once or twice a week and making sure their food was brought from the camp kitchen every day. Their food was better and meatier than the food the inmates received.

Occasionally, I would clean Göth's Mercedes car. He also had a stable full of horses, but Ukrainian guards looked after them. When Göth was not in the villa, I would still have to feed the dog but would return to work at the Bürstenbinderei during the day. I would join my father at the worskhop to bore holes in the brushes simply because I wanted to be there in his company. I would also go so that I could help produce a few more handles for the bench people to string, because it was essential to keep the bench people productive or the Germans might kill them.

One night when Göth was away and I had the day off, I went to join my father after feeding the dog. My father was working the night shift, and I was very tired because I was not used to being up so late. I eventually stopped the drilling machine, a simple motor with a chuck at the end of a shaft, and slumped over, half asleep. I was startled awake by a shot, which broke the window behind me. I thought at first that the bullet had been meant for me, but then I saw that one of the foremen had lain down for a nap in the straw (some of our brushes were made from straw and the room was full of it) and he had been shot and killed.

The next day, I told Göth that something terrible had happened at work the night before. He replied that he had returned at night and had wanted to check up on the work camp. When he walked by the workshop and saw "that lazy bum" lying in the hay asleep, he "took care of him." He also said that he had seen me snoozing, but with a smile on his face, added that I was still "useful." Then he walked away. That was how vicious and sadistic that man was.

But I did not always escape harm. My father and I slept on an upper bunk, which was considered a better location than the lower bunks, since straw and dust would fall on the lower bunks during the night. One particular night, the Jewish police lieutenant, Finkelstein, who was the son of a rabbi, came into the sleeping quarters and demanded that we get up as he needed men. He was an outrageous and miserable person and was whipping people to get them up. Accidentally, he hit me as I lay in bed with my father and the end of the whip split my eyebrow. Finkelstein recognized me and knew my position, so I did not have to go with the ousted group. When he saw that I was bleeding from my eyebrow, he took me over to the first aid station himself, apologizing profusely. The wound eventually healed with a scar, which I still have today.

Another time when Göth was away, two SS officers came into the camp. It seemed they had been sent to clear out some of the "less useful" inmates. They arrived at noon when the night shift was in the barracks and the Jewish police forced night-shift workers from several buildings to the *Appellplatz*. I happened to be with my father because of Göth's absence, and we wound up assembled with the others for a selection. The SS officers walked by the columns of men who were gathered, and every so often the fellow in charge would point his whip and say, "Heraustreten" (step out). Then the person he pointed at would be added to a column of men standing separately. There were two obviously religious boys just ahead of me. They had shaved heads but had hidden their *payot*, sidelocks, behind their ears. When the SS approached our group, they pulled both of the boys out to the separate column. As they passed my father and me, they hesitated, noting my father's bald spot. Pointing his whip at my father, the officer in charge said, "Heraustreten." I took a risk and stepped out too.

This particular SS officer did not know about me or my important position in Göth's villa, but I spoke up in perfect German. "The man who just stepped out of the column is essential to production at the Bürstenbinderei. He is the only one who knows how to sharpen the drills used in the manufacturing of brushes." After sizing me up, the German said, "Ja?" He then ordered us both to go back to our original positions in the columns. I was very happy and relieved to have saved my father, because the two truckloads of those selected people went to Auschwitz. Unfortunately, I did not know at the time that I had only helped to extend his suffering.

Some of the prisoners at Plaszow were selected to work outside the camp in various factories. These groups of workers were known as *Kommandos*. My uncle Yechiel Brühand worked as part of a *Kommando* unit in a cable-making factory. Although these *Kommandos* were technically part of the Plaszow camp, the workers were housed where they worked. Sometime in 1943, these *Kommandos* were liquidated. Some of the luckier workers who worked in the Wieliczka salt mines, such as the woman who later became my wife, were sent back to Plaszow. Others, like my uncle Yechiel, were never heard from again.

Speaking Up

I worked for Göth for about a year or year and a half until, one day in the summer of 1944, he told me that he was going to send me and my father to a better camp in Gross-Rosen, Germany. He gave no explanation. A transport was being arranged and we were to be on it. Göth would have been well aware that Plaszow was going to be liquidated over the next year and that the majority of its inmates would be sent to Auschwitz to be killed. I think this is why he sent us. Gross-Rosen had no gas chambers.

There were about two hundred of us, all men, who were loaded onto cattle cars, arriving three days later at Gross-Rosen concentration camp. After stopping at a railroad siding, we marched a few kilometres to the gates of the camp, where an orchestra made up of inmates welcomed us with marching music. We tried to walk as straight as we could through the gate. When most of the marchers were in, the kapos and barracks leaders who had been standing on the sidelines watching us began to yell as they brought out their sticks and whips to beat us. They shouted, "Los, los!" (Get going!)

We were herded into a huge *Appellplatz*, which was empty and well kept. When we had assembled, two SS officers and ten barracks leaders and kapos ordered us to undress. They told us that our valuables were to be turned over at two tables presided over by the SS men. But from what I could see, there was nobody who had valuables after Plaszow. Our old clothes were piled on one side of the *Appellplatz*, and once we had stripped we were assembled again. Before receiving new clothes, we had to undergo an inspection. We were required to bend over, lift up our arms and turn around. A couple of the kapos checked if we had anything hidden in our orifices. Then we were sent into a shower building, where we washed very quickly as the kapos kept hurrying us. We received new striped prisoners' uniforms, but these were not necessarily the right size. Some people were given clothes that were too tight or too big. I managed to get reasonably sized clothing, but my father's trousers were too short for him. He was a tall man and, therefore, had a harder time finding clothes that fit.

That same afternoon we had to assemble outside again and wait. Finally, we saw trucks coming through the gate. All of us had been assigned numbers that were visible on our striped uniforms and the trucks were being loaded according to these. My number, which I believe was 989, was a few digits greater than my father's. Each of the trucks took thirty to thirty-five men, and when the SS man and kapos overseeing us were loading the second truck, they called my father's number but not mine. I was one number too high. Again, I took a risk and addressed the SS man. I told him that I had been working for *Hauptsturmführer* Amon Göth in Plaszow and requested to be allowed to join my father as it had been Göth's intention that we stay together. Luckily for me, the SS man listened and took one man off the truck and sent me instead. That is how both my father and I left Gross-Rosen on the very same day that we arrived.

Late at night, we arrived at a small camp called Falkenberg in the village of Ludwigsdorf. It was a satellite camp under the jurisdiction of Gross-Rosen. My father and I worked side by side in a forested valley between mountains, cutting out squares of soggy turf from the swampy areas. This turf was then stacked, dried and burned in huge tanks attached to the cabs of German trucks that converted it into fuel. Other work groups in our camp were responsible for supplying the military with lumber and spent their days cutting down trees.

The camp was under the jurisdiction of the Organisation Todt and was guarded by only a few SS guards. Todt was a construction and military unit of the Third Reich that supplied the German army with various materials. Todt officers wore a different uniform than the rest of the German army, brown in colour, with special insignia on their sleeves.

Around the camp were two watchtowers and a plain wire fence. The fence was not electrified, but since there was virtually nowhere to go, it wasn't worth trying to escape. We were surrounded by wilderness, and there was no chance of survival in that rugged environment. Even if you survived the long journey to a town, you could not count on any help from the German people.

After a few weeks of working in the swamps, I developed pain in my ankles and knees. One day while in the turf fields, I fell over and could not get up. The SS guard came over and asked what was wrong. Speaking in German, I told him the truth. My father was trying to help me and the guard, not knowing that we were related, told him, "You look healthy enough. When work is over, carry him back to the camp." That is exactly what my father did. At the end of the day, he carried me on his shoulders a couple of kilometres back to the camp.

The camp consisted of about a half a dozen wooden barracks. In one of these buildings there was an infirmary with a recovery area for injured workers with short-term problems. This infirmary was run by Dr. Price, one of the prisoners who had been a doctor in Lodz. My father brought me in to see him, and after examining me, Dr. Price diagnosed my problem as polyarthritis, an acute inflammation of the joints. The infirmary had a very limited supply of medication, but somehow Dr. Price found some ASA, aspirin, which he mashed into a powder and had one of his assistants give me this powder twice a day. As well, Dr. Price appointed another patient, who had a slight wrist injury, to place heated bricks from the pot-belly stove at my feet. While there was still some pain, the heat made my legs feel better. There were six other people in the recovery area at the time with various problems, such as broken limbs, cuts and bruises, but I was probably the longest-staying patient and was there for about two months.

Periodically, someone from the SS would come to the camp to make sure everything was running as intended and check if there were inmates with long-term sicknesses in the recovery area. People who were unable to work were taken away in a truck to be killed, I imagine, in Auschwitz or another death camp. One of these inspections happened while I was still bedridden. Dr. Price claimed our ailments were all short-term problems and when it came to me, he said I'd had a minor accident and would be out in a couple of days. Luckily for me and for Dr. Price, I had had my feet and the bricks covered with a blanket, and the SS did not realize the true nature of my problem. Dr. Price saved me from being taken away.

After a while, somewhere toward the end of 1944, I recovered sufficiently that I could walk with a makeshift cane. Dr. Price took it upon himself to arrange a work assignment for me that I would be able to tolerate and wouldn't require me to leave the camp grounds. I became one of the helpers in the kitchen, peeling potatoes. After a few weeks, I was promoted to head potato peeler. Thousands of potatoes were under my scrutiny. Most of the kitchen workers, except for one, were Hungarian Jewish men. Out of necessity, I learned Hungarian so I could communicate with the cooks and carry out the prep instructions. My job in the kitchen was a benefit to both me and my father. Sometimes I was able to get him an additional bowl of soup or a potato that he could bake later on the pot-belly stove in the sleeping quarters.

One of my memories of Falkenberg is that of my fellow inmate, Yosele, who was assigned to the same building as me. Yosele was about my age, fifteen or sixteen years old. He had a beautiful voice and introduced me to Yiddish songs during the dark nights. One of my favourites was "Avreml der Marvikher" ("Avreml the Thief"). To this day, that song stirs my emotions when I hear it.

∼

The Soviets were liberating Poland and in December 1944 they were nearing our camp, which the Germans did not want discovered. As a result, we were forced to march toward the northwest of Germany. It was wintry and cold. We were a couple of hundred men and had to sleep outside in fields many times. Some nights, though, we were able to find a barn and sleep inside. As we marched along, people weakened and were shot by the Germans if they fell to the back of the line. I was still in some pain, and my father supported me all the way. My arthritis pain is a lifelong condition. My legs are not horrible now, but my hands are and there is no hope of recovery.

After three or four days of marching, we were loaded into open-topped train cars, which usually held coal, and after about three or four days of train travel, we ended up in another camp, Bergen-Belsen. We were unloaded at a railroad siding and marched through the gates.

The barracks that my father and I were assigned to was, I believe, block 26. We were among several hundred people crowded together, sitting practically on top of one another without the ability to lie down. There was no work, and after a few days, we became familiar with the routine. Each day, we prisoners would be chased out to be counted through the single door of the barracks by the barracks leader and his helpers. Ninety-nine per cent of these leaders and their helpers were Jews, with the odd Russian. They behaved just like kapos and would scream at people as they were pushing and shoving them out. If we did not get out fast enough, we would be hit by their whips. When the counting was done, we went back into the barracks.

Getting out every morning was hard for me with my legs in such pain, and my father would sometimes grab hold of me to help me make it out. After a while, my father made an arrangement with one of the barracks leaders, a short and stocky Jewish fellow named David who was from Lodz. Father had previously swallowed a ring, I think, and was able to retrieve it so he could bribe David to take me on as his assistant. From that time on, I was the barracks leader's assistant and my duties were to keep his corner of the building clean. His corner consisted of a single cot and table enclosed by boards and blankets. As his assistant, I did not have to go outside each morning with the others, poorly dressed in the winter cold, to wait an hour to an hour and a half for the head count. I was allowed to stay inside until the counting had actually begun.

Another of my privileges as David's personal aide was that I got to sleep at the entrance to his cubicle, which gave me a larger area to recline in than the other prisoners had. David assigned me this location not for my benefit but for his own security, since it made sure that no one would enter his cubicle while he slept. My father slept only two metres away from me on the floor.

As liberation neared, David became more disagreeable and demanding. My father noticed this and reassured me, saying, "I will fix it up. I will fix it up." Incredibly, he still must have had some hidden valuables with which to bribe David, because my situation lasted for several more weeks, until liberation.

Meanwhile, people in the camp were dying by the thousands of starvation and typhoid. My father too was sick. On April 12, 1945, just three nights before we were liberated, I heard my father calling out my name. I crawled over to where he was lying, and he pointed up at the small window just below the eaves. There were several of these narrow windows, which were probably for ventilation, but we could see daylight through them during the day.

My father whispered to me, "Can you see?"

I looked up and saw what looked like lightning in the dark sky. The flashes kept reoccurring, and he said to me, "Stay alive! Stay alive, because the end is near. Can you see? Can you see?"

I returned to my spot near David's cubicle entrance and went to sleep. Those were the last words my father spoke to me. He had been practically half-dead for about a week or so, and that night, perhaps only minutes later, my father died of starvation. He was forty-two years old.

I only learned what had happened at the next morning's head count when I saw my father being dragged out with the other dead bodies. The bodies were taken to a pit behind the barracks and dumped on top of others that had been accumulating. They were eventually covered over with earth, but I did not see my father buried. After learning of his death, I became almost comatose and have no memory of the next several days.

Rebirth

When I came to, it was probably a day or two after we were liberated by the British on April 15, 1945. Two survivors, Malinger and Sternberg, who were from Krakow and had been in Plaszow with my father and me, recounted to me what had happened. They also explained to me that the British troops were looking for someone who understood English.

Malinger told the British about me and pointed me out to them. I recall being shaken by someone who turned out to be a British soldier, and he was asking me, "Do you speak English? Do you speak English?" He kept shaking me, but when I saw his uniform, I was frightened and thought he might be a German. But, finally, thanks to my English lessons in Wolbrom, I realized he was speaking English and I nodded my head and said, "Yes."

From that moment on, I was brought back to life. The British took me out of the barracks on a stretcher and placed me in a Bedford ambulance. Then I was taken, still on the stretcher, to a room that resembled a laundry or a kitchen. The medical staff removed my clothes, washed my body and dried me. They dressed me in a new shirt and some military pants. Then I was hooked up to an IV and taken back to the ambulance, where I would spend most of the next few weeks.

In the ambulance, I was examined by a medical staff member and another officer who informed me that my liberators were part of the

VIII British Corps, specifically the 11th Armoured Division. They asked me if I would make announcements for them through the ambulance's loudspeaker and I agreed. We drove back to areas of the old camp and I did just that.

For several weeks, I remained in the ambulance as a patient while making announcements three times a day. The announcements included general instructions for the liberated prisoners about where their food would be served, where to go for disinfection and showers, and how clothing and supplies would be distributed. A doctor saw me at least twice a day and gave me medications for the abdominal problems I was having. They included diarrhea and cramping pain probably due to dysentery, which was prevalent in the camp before liberation. For at least ten days I was fed only through the intravenous drip, but I eventually began to eat soft foods, such as soup and mashed potatoes.

Every day, hundreds of people were still dying from long-term starvation. People would perish because they could not even stand up to walk to the kitchen area. Approximately a week after liberation, the well-intentioned British brought in a military truck filled with cans of Spam, a preserved meat. They dumped the cans on the side of the road between the kitchen and the sleeping barracks, allowing people to help themselves. This turned out to be disastrous. People would eat one or two cans, but their digestive systems, unaccustomed to food, could not cope with the preserved meat, and so they fell ill with pain, cramps and diarrhea. Eventually, most of them succumbed to dehydration and died. Unfortunately, the goodwill and generosity of the British soldiers resulted in tragedy.

After that, the British devised a different approach. They cleared and disinfected one of the larger buildings where, one by one, they brought in those who couldn't walk and placed them on bunks and cots. These patients were then fed appropriately with soups and other easily digested foods.

The British also started the next task: cleaning up the mountains of dead bodies that were beginning to decompose. With bulldozers, they pushed the bodies into large pits that had been dug within the compound. One such pit was located behind the barracks where my father and I had been and I think it was the one my father's body had been dropped into. After piling up the bodies, the British proceeded to spray the mounds with lime or chloride in order to limit odours and prevent the spread of disease.

Eventually, when I was able to walk around and eat regular food, I stopped staying in the ambulance, though I continued to make the daily announcements for which I received instructions from a British officer. This officer told me that the old camp would be completely liquidated and that we survivors would be transferred to a nearby military camp. Each day another barracks of survivors would be transferred from the concentration camp to the new camp where the conditions would be much better.

The new Bergen-Belsen displaced persons (DP) camp, formerly a German training camp known as the Panzertruppenschule, school for training panzer troops, consisted of solid two-storey stone buildings with individual rooms. On one side of a hallway were small rooms that could accommodate between two and four people on bunk beds, and on the other side were large rooms able to accommodate six to eight people. On each floor, right across from the stairwell, were large communal bathrooms where eight people could bathe at once, and which had four enclosed toilets.

Transferring all the liberated inmates to the new camp took about four weeks. When this was done, the British officer said to me, "Thanks old chap, for all you have done for us, but now you'll have to move as well. We will take you to your new building." We were sitting in his Jeep, and I remember turning around to look at the camp where my father was buried among thousands of bodies. I could see the British soldiers equipped with flamethrowers burning the wooden barracks and I watched as the flames destroyed the barracks of Bergen-Belsen concentration camp.

I was driven to Building 89 where I would end up spending almost a year. There I befriended a man named Yumek Zolty from a small town in Poland. He was maybe thirty years old and I was seventeen. We became roommates, and he treated me like a little brother, giving me advice and bringing both our daily rations from the canteen, which served eight buildings. Our daily rations were the same as the British soldiers' daily rations and included cigarettes and chocolate. Yumek also introduced me to his girlfriend, her sister and her two other roommates. These women lived in Building 88, across from ours. My future wife, Bronka Horowitz, was one of these girls, and that is how we met. It was at their room that I ate my first cooked potatoes after the war.

The Bergen-Belsen DP camp expanded as more survivors were brought in and Jewish life had a rebirth there. The camp was mostly run by self-administration. On April 18, 1945, a Jewish Camp Committee had been formed, and they held democratic elections in September. Josef (Yosele) Rosensaft became the leader of the youthful and energetic Central Committee of Liberated Jews. Other members of the committee included Berl Laufer, Paul Trepman and Chaim Poslushny. I remember Yosele Rosensaft as a short man whose actions made him a great man. He would walk around the camp with a pad of paper in his hand, stopping everyone he passed to note down their names and hometowns. He shared this list with other camps to help families reunite. He also initiated the creation of the World Federation of Bergen-Belsen Survivors. He met his future wife, Dr. Bimko, in Bergen-Belsen, and they eventually immigrated to Switzerland and then the United States. He later would become well known as an activist for the State of Israel.

Bergen-Belsen was one of the largest liberated camps and it became steadily more populated as displaced people from the concentration camps of Poland and Germany and other places arrived. They came because Bergen-Belsen was well organized. The Jewish police were established, and soon schools were organized, as well as an orphanage, a yeshiva and, through ORT (Organization for Rehabilitation Through Training), a vocational school. There was a Yiddish theatre, a Zionist newspaper and a good hospital, which had originally served the German military. Later on, in 1946, the British stopped allowing new people to enter the camp and transferred administration to the United Nations Relief and Rehabilitation Administration (UNRRA).

I was still working for the British, which is why Yumek was allowed to bring my rations to me, because I was busy as the official camp interpreter, liaising between the British soldiers and the Jewish police. Both groups had offices in the same administrative building, GB6. Mr. Vilnick was the head of the Jewish police, and messages had to be conveyed between him and a British major. I thought perhaps that the major, a very proper British person, was Jewish too. On many occasions the major offered me goods confiscated from the Germans during the liberation of Bergen-Belsen. I took one thing for myself, a waterproof military watch, which I still have. For my girlfriend and future wife, Bronka, I took another tiny little watch. It was simple and mechanical and had no jewels. It impressed me simply because of its size, not its value.

I was also asked by the British to assist in the Nuremberg Trials. All the Allies were involved in the Nuremberg Trials, and the major and two other officers took me to the American zone of occupation. There, for two or three weeks in an office building, but not at the actual trials, I helped translate the German testimonies into English. After the British brought two of their own translators from England, I was returned to Bergen-Belsen.

Strength to Endure

I think of the Yiddish expression *a mentsh iz a mol shtarker fun ayzn*, a person is stronger than iron. With my father's death, I had lost the last link to my family. And yet, within a few months of that loss, I was able to walk again, to be involved in the world and to live. By keeping busy, I numbed the feeling of all the losses I had endured. Perhaps I was driven not only by an instinct to survive, but also by stubbornness and defiance — a desire to show the enemy that the Jewish people would endure. *Am Yisrael Chai*! The Nation of Israel Lives!

As I continued to gain strength, I became more socially involved. I also inquired, through all available avenues, particularly Yosele Rosensaft's Committee of Liberated Jews, about whether anyone from my family had survived. Tragically, the search turned up nothing.

As life in the camp stabilized, people began to realize they needed more than daily rations and a bed to sleep in. They began to look outside the camp for better food, trading the coffee and cigarettes that formed part of the rations for fresh fruit and vegetables. Eventually, clothing, cameras and watches also became part of the trade. I got acquainted with a fellow survivor named Leo Weinberg, who was a few years older than me. He was a very clever, business-minded person and he suggested we establish an enterprise that would benefit both of us. I was very excited at the prospect of a better life that would allow me to take my girlfriend Bronka to Hamburg or the theatre in Hanover.

Our plan was to start a canteen selling hard-to-come-by goods, such as vegetables, fruit and soda pop. There would be no money involved in the transactions, only bartering and trading goods. Through my connections, I was able to get a large room on the main floor of Building 46 for this purpose. The location was especially convenient since Leo and I now lived on the second floor of the same building. Also, the main floor was accessible to everyone in the camp and was an easy place to unload merchandise.

Our business became known as Cantina 46. Leo managed the business side, and I handled the acquisition and transportation of the goods. We bartered coffee and cigarettes to get a truck and driver for pickups and deliveries, and I would go to Celle, a town about twenty-five kilometres away, to get soda pop from the manufacturers. Our girlfriends, Bronka and Luba, were the salespeople. It became a very successful operation. Competition arose when another canteen, Cantina 43, opened up in a neighbouring building. However, our canteen was the only supplier of soda pop for a long time, something everyone wanted.

Bronka and I decided that we wanted to get married. We had been seeing each other for a few months and had many things in common. Her mother died ten days before liberation, and my father had died only three days before we were freed. We were in the same situation and had been through so much. We were both downtrodden and wanted to start a new life together.

On August 21, 1946, Bronka and I got married. Leo and Luba decided to get married on the same date, which made ours the first double wedding to take place in Bergen-Belsen. The ceremonies were performed by Rabbi Oberlander, a fellow survivor and camp resident, who had been a rabbi in his former life in Hungary. Through my connections, we were able to get access to a large hall that had originally served as a mess hall for German soldiers. We had a regular chuppah, a wedding canopy, made out of a tablecloth and four sticks and got a *ketubah*, the Jewish marriage contract. Our wedding guests included most of the survivors living in Camp 2 (our division of the Bergen-Belsen DP camp), some of the officials we had daily contact with and some of our business associates. Mr. Potok, the gentleman who ran the kitchen, prepared food for the wedding, and pictures were taken by Herr Kote, one of the German fruit and vegetable suppliers for Cantina 46. I still have a few of these photos. Herr Kote also supplied potted palm trees to decorate the wedding hall. The only sad thing about the wedding night was that Bronka's heirloom watch was stolen during the festivities.

At the end of 1947, a miracle happened for Bronka, a joy that was shared with those who knew her and understood the importance of reuniting with lost family. Her brother, Rachmiel Horowitz, was found alive in Italy. He was about to embark on a ship to Israel but, upon hearing that his sister was alive and had gotten married, he travelled back to Germany to reunite with her and meet me, her husband. Then, in the spring of 1948, more of Bronka's family was found. Her uncle, Rachmiel Steinbaum, and his wife, Monia, found out that Bronka was alive in Bergen-Belsen and came to see her. Her uncle had recovered some family heirlooms from a hiding place and gave Bronka her mother's watch and ring. Uncle Rachmiel and Monia set up a home in Memmingen, in southern Germany, and we kept in close contact since Monia was due to have her baby. The night before the birth, I drove to Memmingen. I had a permit for a car available to me whenever I needed it from the Bergen-Hohne training area that was affiliated with the camp. In the morning, I took Rachmiel to the hospital. We arrived in time for the birth announcement — it was a girl. After I returned to Bergen-Belsen, I learned that Bronka's new cousin would be called Lola.

As those of us living in the camp began adapting to normal life after the war, we started thinking about the future. New chapters of organizations such as the Betar movement and Poale Zion sprang up. A few people tried to return to their country of origin, but there was a strong desire among survivors to have a country of their own.

A group called the Jewish Brigade fuelled this desire by encouraging people to make aliyah, immigration to Palestine. Aliyah became an important word in our daily lives, as people started to scheme and plan their departures. But, although Palestine was where most wanted to go, others believed there was a better life to be found in North America.

In the meantime, I was busy with my bartering enterprise. It was a time-consuming job. In 1948, West Germany introduced the Deutsche Mark as its currency. However, coffee and cigarettes still maintained their value as bartering commodities because of their rarity. Many German people had hidden valuables, such as motorcycles and bicycles, during the Nazi occupation, and rather than have these things confiscated, they traded them for coffee, cigarettes and American dollars, which I also dealt in. I spent a lot of time travelling to smuggle items — truckloads of cigarettes and chocolates — from Belgium along the Rhine River into the camp. The items I brought were sold in the camp to people who then traded them outside the camp. Having these small luxuries around allowed the camp community a feeling of normalcy.

In addition, I still had my position as camp interpreter. At one point, I was asked to assist the German authorities in Hamburg to identify a dead man. He was Jewish and had been found in a basement in the Reeperbahn, the city's red-light district, with some documents on his person. It was obvious that he had been killed, since he had multiple wounds. Inquiries were made within the Bergen-Belsen community, and we found a person who claimed to be a relative. Then this person and I, accompanied by a British officer and a German police officer, went to Hamburg to identify the body in the basement. I wondered how the victim had ended up there. Perhaps he had been robbed and then killed to stop the thieves from being identified. The experience rattled me. I stood there with the dead man's relative and realized that we were still in the country where millions of our brethren had been murdered. I remember the relative asking, "When is it going to be enough? When?" We felt we should find a way to leave that country.

Around that time, there was a big change in my life. While my enterprises, both legal and illegal, were doing well, something happened that restored my faith in life on a much deeper level. The lists of survivors that were being compiled by Yosele Rosensaft yielded a positive result, and the committee informed me that they had received a request from a transit camp in Bavaria from a Bela Spiegler who was looking for Avraham Gajer!

When I heard this news, I said goodbye to my wife and, with very little preparation, got into my car and drove to Wasseralfingen, Bavaria. I drove all through the day and late into the evening on difficult, snowy roads to the village. There, I got directions to the transit camp and convinced the guard to escort me to my aunt Bela Spiegler and my cousins, Avraham and Chaim. The reunion occurred in the barracks. There was a moment of great joy followed by a deluge of questions. "What happened to my sisters?" "Where is everybody?" My aunt was the sole remnant of my mother's family and the only adult close to me who had survived the Holocaust. I hadn't seen them since they were shipped off from Lwów to Siberia by the Soviets. They had been in Siberia during the whole of the war and had survived, in part, because of my mother's food packages. It was a sombre and tearful night.

However, in the morning, our spirits were lifted by Avraham and Chaim, who were now twelve and ten years old. They were so excited about coming back with me to Bergen-Belsen that they were already packing. They made Aunt Bela and me realize that we had to get ready for the trip too. When they had gathered their few belongings, Aunt Bela and her boys got into the car with me and we travelled north, back to Bergen-Belsen, a trip that took about ten hours. It was very emotional for my wife to meet my aunt and cousins; there were both happiness and tears.

I found temporary housing for my aunt and her sons in a recreational facility in our block where they had a slightly larger room than the individual couples or singles did. But, within a week or so, I was able to arrange another room for them near us in Building 46. To earn ration cards for herself and the boys, Aunt Bela agreed to become the "hostess" for any temporary guests who had to stay a few days in the Bergen-Belsen DP camp, providing them with food and accommodations in one of the buildings. She was content with this position.

There were a number of young children of elementary school age in the camp who attended an informal school taught by volunteer teachers in a building within one of the blocks that was dedicated for this purpose. Once they were settled in, Avraham and Chaim began to attend school too.

Aunt Bela explained to me how she had found out that I was alive. When she returned to Krakow from Siberia with her two boys, she met a Mrs. Keller, who had been with my father and me in Plaszow. Mrs. Keller felt sure I had survived because of my connection with Amon Göth, who she knew had put me and my father on a transport to Germany. She did not know exactly where we had ended up but knew that those not destined for Auschwitz had a better chance of survival. After that, Aunt Bela started looking at lists and added her name to the lists as well, persisting until she found us.

At the same time, Aunt Bela made efforts to take over and sell my mother's properties in case she did not find us. She had been negotiating with a Soviet officer in the NKVD who had offered her US$20,000 for our property at Aleja Słowackiego 38 in Krakow. But, after speaking to Mrs. Keller, Aunt Bela told the officer that she was not entitled to sell the property at that point. If the sale had been completed, she would have received only a small portion of what the property would eventually be worth. In 1987, it was worth over US$1,000,000. So thanks to Mrs. Keller, Bela and I were able not only to be reunited but to preserve what could be an enormous inheritance.

My aunt and I decided to make sure the property was properly registered in my name. We travelled a few kilometres to a place called Fallingbostel, not far from Bergen-Belsen, where there was a Polish military mission that acted, more or less, as a consulate. We made a declaration verifying that Avraham Gajer was the rightful owner of this property.

The population of the Bergen-Belsen DP camp had started to emigrate. There were those who participated in illegal aliyah, travelling through Italy and France to enter Palestine. The Jewish Brigade, which had been part of the British military, was instrumental in guiding people on this journey. Sometimes tragedy befell the emigrants, as in the well-known case of the *Exodus 1947* emigration ship, which was violently boarded by the British and prevented from reaching its destination; in many cases, those who were stopped were then sent by the British to internment camps in Cyprus. But some people did make it to Palestine and many of those people became the backbone of the Jewish Israeli fighters in the War of Independence in 1948.

My mother's family had always had a strong connection to Zionism. The sisters, including Aunt Bela, had been to Palestine in the 1920s, before they were married, although, unfortunately, they too returned to Poland. Perhaps because of these memories, Aunt Bela decided to take her two sons and make aliyah to Israel, which had been declared an independent state in May 1948.

My wife and I were planning to follow suit but we didn't want to arrive empty-handed. I began bartering cigarettes and other supplies to get furniture and a refrigerator. I had been told that if I could get a truck to Israel, I would be able to make a good living once I arrived. So I went down to Kassel, in the American Zone, and used my connections with the British to buy a surplus, three-axle GMC truck, which I paid for in American dollars. Back in Bergen-Belsen, I had German carpenters build crates in which to ship the truck in pieces. Then we sent the truck, along with the furniture, fridge and other items we thought we would need upon arrival, to Israel.

But just as we were about to embark on our journey, we received a discouraging letter from Aunt Bela. She and her two boys had been living in tents in a camp for *olim chadashim*, newcomers, and struggling daily for food. She strongly advised us not to follow her.

Since I had already shipped the freight, I decided to transfer ownership to my aunt's name. Aunt Bela informed me that the border authorities had confiscated the truck but, in exchange, had allowed the other items to enter the country duty-free. These goods allowed my aunt to sustain herself for a time, acquire a small apartment and barter for other items she needed.

Despite this, Aunt Bela realized she could not support herself and the two boys in the long run. She was working as a wig maker, making *sheitls* for orthodox Jewish women as she and her sisters had done back in Poland, and she could not make ends meet. Because of the difficulty of supporting two sons, Aunt Bela took advantage of an offer from one of the kibbutzim, socialist collective communities, to take in one of the boys.

Kibbutz Afikim became the home of Bela's younger son, Chaim Spiegler. He would eventually become a University of Toronto–educated engineer and the director of one of the plants on the kibbutz. Avraham, the older son, remained with his mother in the small apartment near Tel Aviv. He studied nursing, worked in the Beilinson Hospital in Petah Tikva and eventually became a nursing instructor. Both sons married, had two sons each and lost their wives to cancer at unusually young ages. Each eventually remarried. Chaim had two more sons with his second wife. Avraham did not have any more children. Chaim and Avraham unfortunately succumbed to hereditary heart problems, Chaim at fifty and Avraham at sixty. Their children and grandchildren live in Israel and are still in touch with our family.

Since Aunt Bela had persuaded us not to immigrate to Israel, we decided, along with many other displaced people in Bergen-Belsen, to apply to immigrate to the United States. While awaiting permission to travel, we continued to run the canteen and go about our daily lives. All around us, people were being called in for medical reviews in preparation for immigration. Hundreds of people were processed to go to the United States.

I was acquainted with some brothers by the name of Flantzbaum who often asked me to drive them to Hanover. On one of these trips, we encountered a bicyclist going in the same direction as we were. As I passed him, the rear of my car struck and injured him. We drove him to the nearest hospital in Celle and I told the emergency people what had happened. They asked for my name and license number, which I provided them.

I worried that, with my name and license number in the hospital's possession, I could be taken to court and that would prevent us from being able to immigrate. I felt I had to do everything I could to rush our immigration process.

It was not difficult for me to get into the Rund House, the administration office for the DP camp, and acquire the papers of people who had already left Germany. I took on the identity of a man named Samek Wajsberg, and, since my wife might have been traced by her married name, she took on a new identity as well, using the name Rosa Narocka.

At the time, we did not fully realize the consequences of becoming different people with different backgrounds. For one, we would miss out on the compensation Germany later offered to Holocaust survivors. Since our assumed identities were living people who might also be requesting compensation, we could not apply under their names. Secondly, I would not be able to claim the property I had inherited in Krakow and would, therefore, lose my inheritance. This change of identity also caused many other inconveniences. We now had wrong birthdates, wrong names and everything about us was not really ours. We lost our identities. Although it was a survival strategy, taking on these new identities would become one of my greatest regrets.

We acted as we did because of our survivor mentality. We were young and scared, fresh out of the ashes of the Holocaust and we believed we had to be streetwise and operate with stealth in all our daily activities, in order to survive.

New Names, New World

In 1949, when my wife and I re-registered to immigrate under our new names, we no longer had claim to our marital status and, therefore, would not be called up together for the medical and immigration formalities. I, Samek Wajsberg, was called up a few months after registering and passed. My wife, Rosa Narocka, was called up a few days after me and also passed. We ended up being able to travel on the same transport from Bergen-Belsen to the transit camp in Bremerhaven for the final registration and vaccinations. There, we waited for the next American military boat to transport us overseas. It was customary at that time to use a military boat rather than a passenger boat to transport displaced people to the United States.

To my surprise, after we had been in Bremerhaven a week or so, I was summoned to the US immigration office and asked to leave immediately on the USAT *General Stuart Heintzelman*. The ship lacked an English-speaking translator, and so the crew needed me to interpret. I asked if my "fiancée" could come with me, but they said the boat was already full. They explained that as an interpreter I would be housed in special accommodations so as to be readily accessible when needed, and that, even if we had been husband and wife, we could not stay together there. However, I was assured by someone from HIAS, the Hebrew Immigrant Aid Society, that my fiancée would be on the following transport, the SS *Muriel*, arriving in the United States only a few days after the *Heintzelman*.

The very next morning, I was taken by Jeep to the boat. I was introduced to the first officer, the captain and the radio operator, and we left within an hour. I was shown to a cabin that had just been vacated by two nurses. It was very near the radio room, which was convenient for when I had to make announcements to the passengers. The cabin seemed luxurious to me, and, with two bunks to myself, I couldn't understand why my wife hadn't been allowed to come. But I was told that on a military ship men and women were never allowed to sleep in the same cabin, even if they were married.

Soon after our departure, some people got seasick as the boat was not all that big and it bounced on the waves. Fortunately, I did not suffer from seasickness and was able to perform my duties. These included making announcements in Yiddish, German and Polish about mealtimes, recreation on different decks and other information. About a week after we left, an elderly passenger passed away, and I had to inform the other passengers about the burial service at the back of the boat. I also observed this last rite. It seemed awful to me that someone who had survived the Holocaust would end up being dropped into the ocean. But it was explained to me that this was how anyone who died at sea was buried.

Eight days after our departure, we were informed that, due to weather conditions, our destination had been changed from New York to Boston. While I was making this announcement, I thought about my wife on the SS *Muriel*. I approached the radio operator to ask if I could contact her and the captain gave me permission to speak to Rosa for three minutes. She was very seasick and was being cared for by fellow passengers, whom I later met and became friends with. Hearing her voice was reassuring — I was glad to find out that she was indeed on the SS *Muriel* heading for New York and that we were only a few days apart.

When I disembarked in Boston, Rosa's brother Rachmiel, now Ralph Horowitz, was already in Canton, Ohio, and had asked the local Jewish centre to arrange for Samek Wajsberg and Rosa Narocka to come to Canton too. So, when I landed, there was already someone waiting to put me on a train. The next morning, I arrived in Ohio. I was greeted by Mabel Segrams, the official from the Jewish centre in charge of new arrivals, and Anna Jacobs, who would become like a second mother to me. In the afternoon, I met Morris Jacobs, Anna's husband, and when my brother-in-law, Ralph, returned from his job, he welcomed me joyfully. We ate our first meal together at the Jacobs's house, where I saw for the first time, to my delight, an actual television. In a matter of twenty-four hours, I had reached a free country, arrived at my final destination and was awaiting my wife.

Although high on adrenaline, I eventually collapsed and fell asleep in the same room as my brother-in-law, on the upper floor of the Jacobs's house. I dreamed that I was opening the door for my wife, but instead I sleepwalked and bumped into a window screen, which thankfully prevented me from falling two storeys. This is the only time I know of that I have ever sleepwalked. I think the excitement of the journey and the anticipation of my wife's arrival had overwhelmed me.

A week later, Bronka, now Rosa, arrived in Canton. What a reunion! For several weeks, we lived and ate at the Jacobs's home. With help from Mabel and Anna, I found a job at a Ford dealership called Downtown Motors. I serviced the new cars, which in those days were delivered to the dealership without accessories like radios, antennas and rubber floor mats. I also did minor maintenance jobs, such as checking the oil.

Anna Jacobs knew us only by our documented identities, Sam and Rosa, and so did not know that we were already married. After consulting with us, she arranged for a rabbi to perform a legal American wedding. We had a small ceremony in the rabbi's home and became Mr. and Mrs. Sam Weisberg, which was how we now spelled our new name in America. From then on, we had two marriage certificates.

As "newlyweds," we moved in to a fourplex (a house with four separate apartments) at 1103 Walnut Avenue Northeast, which was fairly close to the Jacobs's home. Anna was always very helpful, providing cooking and baking advice and helping out with various other household needs. She helped Rosa get a job in the stockroom of the Stark Dry Goods department store. That gave Rosa an opportunity to learn English. Before long, I was able to get a better-paying, unionized job as a machinist, making tools and dyes at the Babcock Printing Press. We became close not only with Anna and Morris, but also with their son, Ronny, and their daughter, Elaine.

Now that it felt like our lives were normalizing, we began to think about starting a family of our own. Back in Europe, we had not wanted to bring a new life into the horror that had consumed the continent. We revisited that decision, and Rosa became pregnant. Around the same time, we started the process of applying for American citizenship. After much discussion as to whether we should come forward about having changed our names, we decided that there was too much at stake if the government was not sympathetic. We filed our citizenship applications and continued our lives under our assumed identities.

As other refugees arrived in Canton, Rosa and I became the unofficial welcoming committee, acting as interpreters for those who didn't speak English. Some of these families became our close friends. We used to gather on the front porch of our apartment with the Zelkers and the Bellalis, who had come from Greece. Slowly but surely, everyone found a place to live and a job. I even reunited with Yosele, the young man who had taught me songs at the Falkenberg concentration camp. He had immigrated to Canton because his uncle was living there and ended up marrying his cousin. Sadly, he later committed suicide.

As the months went by, Rosa became more visibly pregnant and took a leave of absence from her job at the department store. Anna kept a careful watch over her and, on March 25, 1952, finally checked Rosa in to the Aultman Hospital. I was told that the birth was still far off. I was restless, so I returned home and decided to occupy myself with something useful. I climbed up onto our roof to install an antenna for our first television set. I was nearly done when Anna pulled in to the driveway and yelled up at me that my wife had gone into labour. I was so shaken that I almost fell off the roof! I arrived just in time for the delivery but had to wait in the waiting room, since in those days the father was only allowed in after the baby had been born. Rosa was in a room with four people and she smiled at me as a nurse brought in a wrapped-up bundle — my lovely new daughter.

A few days later, that bundle of joy and my wife came home. I made my brother-in-law, Ralph, drive his new, two-tone, green 1952 Ford in front of us as a safety buffer as we made our way back from the hospital. I wanted to make sure no accident would befall us while driving with our precious cargo. With the help of "Grandma" Jacobs and our next-door neighbour Julia, my wife became an expert at diapering and bathing a baby. Rosa was so enthused with her new charge and the accompanying responsibilities that she even ironed the diapers.

Cantor Rakoff and his wife helped to arrange a time for our daughter's official Hebrew naming. Our daughter was named Esther Shaiva in Hebrew and Estelle Sharon in English. The names derive from my mother's name, Esther Etel, and Rosa's mother's name, Alta Shaiva.

My brother-in-law, Ralph, who was still a bachelor, became adept at holding, diapering and looking after Sharon. He was much better with the baby than I was, since I was afraid that she would break. He was so good at caregiving that we even, eventually, entrusted him to babysit her.

We kept in touch with our surviving family — my aunt Bela and her two sons in Israel, as well as my wife's uncle Ralph and aunt Monia Steinbaum and their daughter Lola, who now lived only a few hours away in Detroit, Michigan. I remembered Lola's birth on that cold winter morning in Memmingen, Germany, and contemplated how astonishing it was that she was now a young woman.

We also kept in touch with fellow survivors from Bergen-Belsen.

Among them was Morris Grossman, who had been a close associate of mine. He was living in Toronto, Canada, and invited us to visit him there. On one of our trips to Detroit to see the Steinbaums, we crossed the Ambassador Bridge into Windsor, Canada, and then kept driving to visit the Grossmans in Toronto. During our stay, Morris explained that he had bought a business that rented out washers to apartment complexes. He was not knowledgeable about the maintenance or running of the machines and suggested that, because of my mechanical abilities, I move to Toronto and assist him. This was a more attractive job prospect than what was available to me in Canton. Since Grandma and Grandpa Jacobs were planning a move to California to be nearer their daughter, there was very little to keep us in Ohio.

The Grossmans took us to a vacation area known as Jackson's Point, on Lake Simcoe, where Morris made a daring suggestion. He wanted me to leave my wife and daughter in Canada, return to Canton to pack up our belongings and drive back north. We were impressed by certain pleasantries in Canada, including the Lord's Day Act, which mandated that businesses closed on Sundays. In general, the pace of life in Canada seemed slower and less stressful than in the United States. Also, the Canadian dollar was sometimes worth more than the American dollar. Rosa and I talked it through and decided to take him up on this plan. So I left Rosa and Sharon and drove back down to Canton alone.

The only downside to this decision was that we would be leaving Ralph. He was not pleased about this, but he understood the advantages for us. Eventually, though, Ralph decided he wanted to be with his family and, about a year later, followed us to Toronto. In Toronto, Ralph married Edith Hoffman and had three daughters: Anna, Lily and Susie. He joined Morris Grossman's brother, Nathan, in the laundry business and eventually struck out on his own, starting Modern Laundry on Dupont Street.

Ralph helped me pack our belongings into a four-wheel trailer hooked up to my Oldsmobile and we said goodbye. Even though I was transporting all our possessions, when I crossed the border at Fort Erie, all I had to do as an American citizen was fill out a form declaring what I was bringing into Canada.

Our first accommodations in Toronto were on Arlington Avenue near the Grossmans' home. I started my new career with Automatic Laundries Limited in 1955, learning the trade from more experienced washing machine mechanics. I serviced Morris's coin-operated washing machines in sixty locations, as far east as 1600 Kingston Road and as far west as Prince Edward Drive in Etobicoke. The washing machines were mostly wringer washers, though there were a few luxury automatic tumbler washers by Bendex. The wringer washer cost $0.10 for 20 minutes or $0.25 for an hour. The automatic Bendex would do a cycle for $0.25. I spent twelve to fourteen hours a day driving all over town to repair and service the machines. As the business grew, I trained another man, Eddie Wolkesh, to help service the machines and enlisted Rosa to take customer calls and dispatch the mechanics to their destinations.

Eventually, we modernized the equipment and began to service dryers as well. In the beginning, if a machine needed serious servicing, I would take it to my workshop in the basement of our home on Pinewood Avenue, where we moved three months after we came to Toronto. But as the business became more successful, the shop moved to the garage of Morris's new house, and, finally, Automatic Laundries Limited got its own shop on Dufferin Street. By that time, I had two mechanics assisting me, Eddie and Tommy Michaleros. Tommy and his wife, Vera, became lifelong friends of ours.

On April 3, 1956, we finally had another baby, our beloved son, Stanley Max. His Hebrew name was Shlomo Meyer: Shlomo after Rosa's father, Aaron Shlomo, and Meyer after my father, Eli Meyer. We called him by his second name, Max.

My wife's dearest friend, Gucia Lederman (a childhood classmate and fellow survivor of the Holocaust), lived in Toronto and had come over to babysit Sharon while Rosa was in the hospital. In a picture taken of Max's homecoming, Sharon, who was then four years old, is standing on the porch of our home at 126 Pinewood Avenue, holding the door open in welcome. She had been awaiting our arrival. Almost at once, Sharon began to play big sister and "little mother." Max's bris, circumcision, was performed by Dr. Isadore Katz in our house. Friends and fellow survivors came to share the celebratory food we had prepared and to join in the happiness of our expanding family.

In Toronto there was an organization called the Radomer Society, based out of a building on Beverley Street. The membership originally consisted of Jewish people who had arrived in Canada in the early 1900s from the city of Radom, Poland, who wanted to avoid serving in the Polish military and came to create a better life in Canada. They raised funds to help those still left in Radom. One of the ways they helped was by purchasing a cow so that Jews in the Radom hospital could have milk. It was not strictly necessary that a person be from Radom to join the society; I became a member, as did Harry Goldman, Henry Rosenbaum and Shia Koperwas — all newly arrived survivors. They wanted the existing society to do more and they approached me with the suggestion to organize the survivors now living in Toronto to help our brethren in Israel through tough times. As a result, we formed a new group called the B'nai Radom, the Sons of Radom.

In addition to sending funds to Israel, the B'nai Radom helped erect a memorial monument at the Dawes Road Cemetery inscribed with the names of Holocaust victims from Radom, Poland. As a special favour, in recognition of my participation in the B'nai Radom, my parents' names, Esther Etel and Eli Meyer Gajer, were also included on the monument. The unveiling of the Dawes Road Memorial Monument on September 2, 1962, still stands out in my mind. It involved a procession with a police escort, an open convertible with Beth Radom delegates, flags of both Canada and Israel, and other cars with Beth Radom members, who travelled from Bathurst Street and Reiner Road to the Dawes Road Cemetery. The monument is still being maintained, and annual services are held to commemorate the victims of the Holocaust. Descendants of those victims and their families usually attend the ceremonies at the monument site on the date of the liquidation of the Radom ghetto.

An understanding had developed between the Radomer Society and the B'nai Radom, and they had begun to co-operate. One of their shared goals was to build a synagogue. The Radomer Society sold the property on Beverley Street and obtained a parcel of land at 18 Reiner Road, where the Beth Radom Synagogue was built in 1962 by Radomer survivors Harry Goldman and Isaac Garfinkel.

The opening of the synagogue on Reiner Road was a joyous occasion. The Beth David Synagogue lent one of their Torahs for the event. Most of the B'nai Radom members became members of the Beth Radom Synagogue. The first president of the Beth Radom Synagogue was Sam Rosenbaum, an original founder of the Radomer Society in the 1900s and uncle to my friend Henry Rosenbaum. Other notable people who aided in the development of the Beth Radom were Isaac Green, Solly Kates, Benny Hoffman, Abie Glass and Abie Rosen.

As the synagogue membership expanded, the need for religious leadership became apparent, especially during the High Holidays. There was some opposition to the idea of hiring a rabbi, since some people preferred to have member-led prayers. But after a while, Cantor Landy was hired as a Torah reader and *chazzan* (cantor), and he eventually became certified as a rabbi — the Beth Radom Synagogue's first.

The synagogue had a brotherhood and a sisterhood to raise funds and run social functions. My wife and I both served as presidents of the sisterhood and brotherhood, respectively, at different points in time. Membership continued to increase, and Beth Radom became a well-known synagogue in Toronto, continuing in memory of the victims of the Holocaust in Radom, Poland, and elsewhere.

A Bar Mitzvah Abroad

As the Jewish population of Toronto grew, Jewish people started to move further north, first north of Eglinton Avenue and then even further north of Wilson Avenue. In 1962, my wife and I became part of this pattern when we bought a house in the Jewish neighbourhood of Bathurst Manor at 227 Acton Avenue. Our new home allowed each of our children to have their own bedroom, and the neighbourhood offered a choice of Jewish schools. We decided on the school located at the Beth Emeth. Our High Holiday walks to the Beth Radom Synagogue were also shorter than before.

After the move to Bathurst Manor, I became friendly with a group of Radomers who were builders, Richard Birnenbaum, Isenberg, and Sam Katzman. Together, we formed a company called Promenade Builders, which was involved in small projects, such as semi-detached homes and single homes. We ran the company out of an office in my basement and slowly it began to turn a profit. My job was to expedite finding parcels of land to buy, sell or build on.

In addition to working for Promenade Builders, I also had a job with Stan Vine Construction. Stan Vine was a landsman, a person from the same town as me, as he was also from Chorzów. He sought me out because my father had helped his family before the war. Stan's mother had been widowed and my father helped finance her children's education. In Toronto, Stan hired me to manage hundreds of apartment units and several shopping plazas, including the Bathurst Manor Plaza at Wilmington and Overbrook where our office was. Managing the buildings was very time-consuming, and the attention I paid to my work meant that I missed out on spending time with my children as they were growing up, since my wife took care of our home life. I regret not being able to share in that.

The years went by. During the summers, my wife and children would vacation at Jackson's Point, and I would sometimes join them on weekends. I enjoyed fishing with Sharon, who liked to accompany me. Max did not like to fish and stayed on shore with his mother.

In 1969, as Max approached his thirteenth birthday, we began making plans for his bar mitzvah. Aunt Bela was still living in Israel, and we had always wanted to visit her and see the Jewish nation. Rosa and I decided to combine the events into a "bar mitzvah pilgrimage" for our family, along with our friends and my partners, the Isenbergs and the Katzmans. On June 15, 1961, El Al, an Israeli airline, had broken the world record for the longest nonstop commercial flight when it flew a 707 airplane from New York to Tel Aviv. We flew down to New York from Toronto in order to take the nonstop flight to Israel for Max's bar mitzvah.

It is hard to describe how it felt to board the El Al flight. I had an overwhelming sense of being part of a nation, of returning to a place that had been bereft of its Jewish people for thousands of years. The plane took off late at night, and as we flew into the sunrise, a group of Lubavitchers, members of an Orthodox, Hasidic movement, encouraged passengers to join them in davening, praying. I felt a profound sense of oneness, of commitment to our Jewish identity and to the journey we were undertaking. I don't think my wife or I slept for even a minute of that flight. We talked about the bar mitzvah plans and about our family in Israel, speculating about what arrangements Aunt Bela might be making for the festivities.

We landed in Israel the next morning. As we left the plane, we were surprised to see a military Jeep at the foot of the ramp waiting for us. Two soldiers were in the front seat of the Jeep, a woman and a man holding a huge bouquet of flowers were in the back. As we approached, the couple in the back seat came out of the Jeep and presented Rosa with the bouquet. They introduced themselves as Avraham and Ahuva Rozenzweig, the sister-in-law and brother-in-law of my cousin Avraham Spiegler. Our entire bar mitzvah entourage was escorted through security without any delays — passports were stamped and we passed through. Avraham Rozenzweig owned the gas station near the airport, and we suspected that, because of his connections with the airport staff, they let us pass without the intense scrutiny others entering the country had to undergo.

The bar mitzvah guests went their own way, and my family and I were driven by the Rozenzweigs to Aunt Bela's apartment in Bnei Brak. The welcome was emotionally overwhelming.

After we recovered somewhat from our jet lag, we began to concentrate on the bar mitzvah plans again. In the evening, my cousin Avraham stopped by and told us about some cousins of my mother and aunt, the Silbermans. Mr. Silberman had already initiated arrangements to have Max's bar mitzvah ceremony at the synagogue on Bograshov Street, an old and prestigious synagogue in downtown Tel Aviv.

Our Max did his aliyah, call to the Torah, and *lained*, reading, quite well, and we were all very proud. When the prayers were done, the rabbi called me over to congratulate me and to convey a "well done" to the rabbi who had taught Max his *parsha*, Torah portion, and his *brachot*, blessings. Since it was Shabbat, we did not have music or candlelight at the reception. Instead of candles, we used long-stemmed carnations to honour certain individuals from Toronto and Israel; the honouree would place a flower into the large birthday cake.

The joyous event was celebrated with people we knew from Toronto and Israel, including people we had not seen in a long, long time and even people we had never met. Rosie Levy, the daughter of one of our Toronto friends, hitchhiked from a kibbutz on the Golan

Heights to be with us. It was heartwarming to know that people went to such effort to join us on one of the happiest occasions of our lives. The singing, the food, the people, the speeches and the laughter made it an amazing and successful event.

The next morning, we travelled to Jerusalem where we davened at the Western Wall. Max put on his *tefillin* in this holy environment. Aunt Bela showed us the place where my parents' HaSharon café used to be, and we later drove north to see my other cousin, Chaim, and his wife, Ruth, in Kibbutz Afikim. We had an amazing time at the kibbutz and celebrated Passover there. The seder night included a staged children's chorus and instrumental music, including "Ma Nishtana," which was recorded for use on TV. It was a different experience than we were used to.

After we left Afikim, we travelled back south to Jerusalem. Since we had arrived in Israel only a little while after Sharon's birthday, our family went to a nightclub in Jerusalem called the Cave to celebrate. One of our friends got the band to play "Happy Birthday" and a waiter came over with a bottle of champagne, gifted to us by a neighbouring table whose occupants were also from Toronto. They were the Tepermans and ran a company called Teperman Wrecking. I was moved by the generosity of the moment.

In moments like these — the warmth of the bar mitzvah celebration and the joy of revisiting my parents' dreams in the Jewish homeland — I have been able to find some solace from the trauma of my experiences. I still think of Israel as the home of our dreams and of the people there as the ones who rose from the ashes. We were witnesses to Israel's existence, to her people's growth and to her prosperity.

Epilogue: Carrying the Torch

When we returned to Canada, we took up our usual routines of work, school, home and friends. Our lives flourished, grew and prospered on this side of the ocean as well. Our daughter, Sharon, was a hardworking and successful student. She excelled at everything she put her mind to: creative arts, sports, drama, music, religious youth groups and academics. As a student, she won many awards, including a National Research Grant for her research on genetics as a master's student at the University of Western Ontario. During her high school years, she met her *beshert*, her heart's choice, Aaron Jesin. They wed in August 1973 and lived in London, Ontario, while he completed his medical degree.

Then, with Ahuva, their first child, in tow, they returned to Toronto, where Aaron set up a family practice with Sharon as his assistant. He also began to work as a *mohel*, circumciser, and performed many thousands of circumcisions on Jewish baby boys over his career. Sharon and Aaron lead a *dati*, religious, life and have six wonderful children, each a gem and a reminder of the six million who perished. The fact that these children are now marrying and having children of their own is a testament to the rebirth that has happened.

Our son Max grew up into a real mensch, a fine person. He worked hard at everything he did. He was a generous person and, for his means, a philanthropist. He graduated from Seneca College with a technical degree and was hired by the Lytton Appliance Company. He met his *beshert*, Lynda Tully, in Toronto, and they wed in 1983.

They had a loving but brief life together, as Max was struck down by Hodgkin's disease. His struggle, pain and suffering were things no parent, least of all a survivor of the Holocaust, should have to witness and are among the things the Almighty will have to explain later.

Our six grandchildren bear the names of people lost in the Holocaust and of our son lost to Hodgkin's disease: Ahuva Leah, Maytal Mira, Aliza Chaya, Yehezkel Moshe, Raphael Chaim and Shlomo Meir Yirmiyahu. Some of them live in Israel and others in the United States. They have now given us eighteen great-grandchildren — the eighteenth, my "chai" great-grandchild, was born in 2018 — and I hope for many more. To them I pass this torch, asking them to carry it high, to carry it proudly and, most importantly, to never forget.

A LASTING LEGACY
Johnny Jablon

Preface

I am writing this memoir for two reasons: The first and most important is to ensure that nobody can deny the Holocaust happened, since I, a thirteen-year-old boy when the war started, witnessed the horrors of six concentrations camps and lost my whole family. I can testify that it happened.

The second reason is that no matter how bad it was (and to tell the truth, I am not sure if I can really describe the horrors), there was always somebody trying to help, giving me a ray of hope and the will to survive.

I will document my memories the way I remember things happening.

What I Remember

I was born as Jan Rothbaum in Krakow, Poland, on January 20, 1926. Krakow is a beautiful city, over a thousand years old, from which kings ruled for centuries. In medieval times, the city was surrounded by high walls to keep invaders out, and in the early nineteenth century, when they began to decay, most of the walls were dismantled and replaced by a beautiful green belt known to this day as Planty Park.

I lived with my parents, Dora Rothbaum (née Ormian) and Schulem Rothbaum, and my two brothers, Roman (Romek) and Joseph, right across from the park, at 9 Zamenhofa Street. My mother took us to the park almost every day, where she met her sisters and friends and I played with my cousins. The ladies all wore such beautiful hats, almost as if they were competing with each other.

In the summer of 1936, a public swimming pool was opened in Błonia Park, an area outside the old centre of Krakow. I was ten years old and went to the pool with my brothers, Romek, who was thirteen, and Joseph, seven. Romek threw me in the water, and I started to swim. What a thrill! I learned how to swim just like that. Little did I know that the memory of that wonderful feeling would help me through horrors I could not have imagined.

In 1939, I finished my sixth year of school and wrote the entrance exams for the *gimnazjum* (high school), which I was to start in September. But first, my parents sent me to summer camp in Rytro, a resort town in the Tatra Mountains not far from the famous resort Krynica. My aunt Rozia (one of my mother's five sisters) and her children were vacationing not far from the camp, and my cousins visited me often. We had a terrific time together during that wonderful summer.

Why do I remember that summer so well all these years later? Those memories helped me survive the terrible times that were to come. Every time I was beaten in the concentration camps, which was often, I was able to disconnect myself and go back to the joyous times of that summer.

We were supposed to return to Krakow on the first of September, but the week before, our counsellors became very nervous and there were rumours about war. We packed up early. Our train going home took much longer than usual because some of the bridges had already been sabotaged, and when we finally arrived, on August 31, I learned my parents and brothers had been waiting at the station for hours, very anxious to see me.

The next day, September 1, the German army invaded Poland. A bomb fell close to the Krakow railway station, which our family lived near. We ran to our aunt who was living in the centre of the old town not far from the Sukiennice, the Cloth Hall, now part of the National Museum. That was the day our lives changed. Suddenly, there was not enough food; we had to wait in long lines to buy bread or anything else, and things were about to get worse.

By September 6, Krakow was fully occupied by the German army, and persecution of the Jewish population began, organized mainly by Nazi officers. Jews were being picked up on the streets and forced to do degrading work. One of my cousins, Emanuel, who was my brother Romek's best friend, was caught just a few days after the Germans came in and was made to clean toilets with his own shirt. But I think that experience saved his life, because the next day he escaped to the USSR, where he joined the Polish army. He was the only other member of my family to survive the war. Afterward, he went to Israel, where he became a colonel in the army and was eventually appointed a military attaché in Ethiopia.

In December 1939, the entire Jewish population was forced to wear armbands bearing the Star of David. It was almost impossible to go out on the street and not be picked up by the Germans and sent to clear snow from the roads, sometimes for a couple of days without a break. Every Jewish family had to send people to work.

I went with my father and Romek one day to clear snow. We were surrounded by Germans who beat us with whips and yelled, "Schnell, schnell, verfluchte Juden!" (Fast, fast, you cursed Jews!) They hit my father, who was breaking ice with a pick, and yelled to us, "Keep working, keep working! Don't look up!" The work went on until the middle of the night, when we were finally allowed to go home.

On another day we were sent to work at the infamous Montelupich prison. There, we were made to dig a large ditch in the frozen ground, and God forbid we should stop for a second; we would have been beaten to death by the Germans. I was sure we were digging our graves, that at any given moment we'd be shot, but after we had dug the first ditch, we were ordered to close it, fill it in. Dig and fill, dig and fill, over and over again.

At least our family was still living together in our house on Zamenhofa Street, as we had before the war started, hoping still that somehow we would survive, together.

On March 3, 1941, the Krakow ghetto was established in Podgórze, a district across the Vistula River in the southern part of the city. In the days before we were forced to move there, word of the mass relocation made its way to the countryside, and thousands upon thousands of Polish peasants came to the city to pillage and take whatever they could from the Jews. We were able to exchange a few things for a wheelbarrow, load it with whatever we could and wheel it through the streets of Krakow, across the bridge over the river and into the ghetto. Along the way we were laughed at and insulted by the Polish population. They seemed happy to see us suffer.

In the ghetto, my family was very lucky to get a one-room apartment. It was small, but at least we were all together. The Germans exploited the cheap labour available from the imprisoned population by establishing several factories, both inside and outside the ghetto walls.

I think the best way for me to describe life in the ghetto here is to include an excerpt from a translation of a letter I wrote to my uncle in Palestine while I was in a displaced persons (DP) camp in Linz, Austria. The letter is dated July 6, 1946, one year after the war.

Dear Uncle,

I am writing a second letter to you, in which I will describe the last moments with my parents.

As you probably know, before the war we were living in Krakow, on Zamenhofa Street. We were very well off; my older brother, Roman, started to work in the office and I was about to start the first year of gimnazjum. *Everything was all right. We were active members of our society, when all of sudden war broke out and the Hitler regime took over. It killed all our dreams and plans for the future.*

We did not know what the future held for us.

First, they threw out all the Jews from the gimnazjum, *our father lost his business (because it was taken away from him) and Romek lost his job. Next we had to wear a yellow Star of David, on which was written* Jude, *and everybody had to do manual work, usually digging ditches, shovelling snow from the street. We were not allowed to go to the parks or walk through the main streets. But this was only the beginning.*

On March 20, 1941, a decree was issued that all the Jews from Krakow were to be transferred to the ghetto, which was created on the other side of the Vistula River in Podgórze, in the vicinity of the streets

Rękawka, Lwowska, Plac Zgody and Rynek Podgórski. The ghetto was surrounded by a very high brick wall so that nobody could escape from it. Any so-called citizen of this so-called Jewish state had to have a valid identification document and was obliged to work for the Germans. We were being beaten, our teeth broken, and many times we came back from work with broken bones and other injuries. But this was nothing, until the first Aktion came, in which we lost Romek.

And then came the bloody day of October 28, 1942, which I will never forget for as long as I will live. It was a beginning in my life and the day that I changed from a child to a serious man who survived four years in many concentration camps, and who survived only with the thought of revenge on the bloody German murderers.

Now I will describe that one day:

We got up that morning to go to work, when all of sudden we heard our mother screaming as she looked through the window (our window was facing outside of the ghetto). We all ran to look and we saw what we had been afraid of for quite a while. The ghetto was surrounded by SS troops specially trained for "liquidations" (killings) of Jews. What the word Aktion means we now know very well. It means hundreds of dead people and thousands taken for transport to an unknown destination (later on we found out that the unknown destination was the crematoria in Bełżec, Treblinka, Majdanek and many others, where we lost millions of our brothers).

You have to forgive me, dear uncle, for the chaos in my writing, but when I start to remember the horrible times, then I can write only the way that I remember. Well, let us continue.

We are sitting and huddling together in one room, because we're not allowed to go out, and listening to any noises coming from outside where, in the meantime, it was very quiet (quiet before the storm). Mother is crying very quietly; she knows that something very terrible is coming. We are trying to assure her that everything will be okay. I felt like a grown-up person, although I was only sixteen years old.

Our thoughts were with you in far-away Palestine, where most likely you had no idea what was going on here.

All of sudden, we start to hear a few shots and then a whole volley. It had started! We hear crying, yelling, moaning, and we know for sure that there must be many dead. Mother is crying together with our small cousin, who was living with us with his mother, Aunt Sally.

Then we hear heavy steps of the SS coming to our door. They are here! We are sitting together hugging each other, waiting for something terrible to happen. Then, the steps stopped right in front of our door ... a big bang and they are in. Sadistic faces with sadistic smiles slowly coming toward us.

One of them gives a yell: "Now I'll deal with these damn Jews!"

One of the beasts started to beat my dearest mother. Then something snapped in me. Blindly, and with the most hate I could muster to the animal who could raise a hand to my mother, I threw myself on him with the fist. Me, a sixteen-year-old boy, trying to fight the big German.

I can still hear his sadistic laugh together with my mother's scream. Then I felt a blow to my head and I lost consciousness. I was left for dead. They left me bleeding on the floor. In the evening, a few of the boys, who were working in the Gestapo headquarters (cleaning the toilets), found me on the floor. They said that I was very lucky (lucky, who in few minutes had lost everybody). I did not cry. I swore to myself that if I survive, I will seek revenge. Well, I survived, but I haven't yet seen my revenge.

After the Aktion *in which I lost everybody, my parents, brothers and the whole family, they took me to a concentration camp in Plaszow, where I was for one and a half years. In February 1944 I was sent to the famous Auschwitz, then Mauthausen, Melk, Gusen, and finally Gunskirchen, where I was liberated by US soldiers on May 4, 1945.*

This letter describes October 28, 1942, the day I lost my whole family. I remember every second even now, all these years later.

At that time, we had been living together in one room with another family, the Joachisman family — a father with two daughters and their aunt. One of the daughters, Dysia, was about my age. It was love at first sight for me when we met. Dysia was the one who constantly told me that we had to survive so we could help punish the guilty ones. After the war, I learned from friends of hers that Dysia did survive, though I don't know what happened to her. Her family did not survive.

After my mother, father, two brothers, about sixteen aunts, uncles and many cousins, along with dear friends like the Joachismans, were killed by the Germans, I was living all alone in the ghetto. In the beginning, I worked for Oskar Schindler, at his Emalia (enamel) factory just outside the ghetto walls. It was an excellent job, but after a short time I was replaced by somebody else, who most likely bribed someone to get in. I then worked with about twelve other Jewish people in a lumberyard outside the ghetto walls. I was doing all kinds of jobs, like piling lumber and cleaning; I was later trained to sharpen the saws, which was quite a good job.

On January 15, 1943, I was close to turning seventeen. We were leaving the ghetto for the lumberyard when we were surrounded by the OD (Jüdischer Ordnungsdienst, Jewish Order Service, better known as the Jewish ghetto police) and forcefully taken to an empty building, where we were kept for some hours before being sent to the Plaszow forced labour camp.

The Horror of the Camps

If there is a way to describe hell, it would be the Plaszow forced labour camp, but I am not sure anyone could actually communicate the horrors of that place.

Plaszow was a suburb of Krakow and where the Jewish cemetery was located. The camp was built on top of the cemetery, and the headstones were used to pave the roads. The site was a hilly, rocky area stretching down to swamps full of malaria-ridden mosquitoes. Those hills were levelled and the swamps drained at the heavy cost of Jewish blood.

The camp was surrounded by rows of barbed wire charged with high-voltage electricity — enough to cause instant death to humans. Ground security was reinforced from watchtowers, where Ukrainian guards were posted with machine guns ready to fire.

The walls of the barracks where we lived were built of thin, ill-fitting boards. Wooden crates placed next to each other served as beds. There were no mattresses, no heat, no water. The worst thing was having to relieve ourselves at night; running to the latrine in the dark, we could very easily be shot by the Ukrainians.

Not far from the barracks was the *Appellplatz*, main square, where we had to assemble every morning for roll call. This was also the place prisoners were beaten, shot, hanged and made to suffer by any number of other means. Behind the barracks was a mass grave in which thousands of men, women and children were buried. A little farther away were two more mass graves. One of them was on a hill known as Hujowa Górka, Hujar's Hill, named after one of the most vicious SS officers, Albert Hujar. Every day the hill served as the execution site for Jews selected as unfit to work. Before their execution, the condemned had to undress and be examined for gold teeth. At the orders of the killers, any gold teeth were removed by workers before the victims' bodies were thrown into the deep pit.

Close to the women's block was the *Revier*, the living quarters for the sick, beside which was a hospital. The head of the hospital was a Jewish inmate of the camp named Dr. Leon Gross, appointed by the Nazis, who regularly demanded the doctor list the patients who were too sick to work — to be murdered. He had to deliver. He listed the very old and the very sick, but at the same time he saved a few lives, including mine. After the war, Dr. Gross returned to Krakow, was put on trial, found guilty of collaboration and consequently hanged in 1946. Although he'd saved some lives, he had also assisted the Nazis in their efforts.

When I arrived at Plaszow on January 15, 1943, the commander of the camp was an SS officer named Franz Müller, who was responsible for the killing of the first Jewish foreman, Tobiasz Katz. I believe that Katz was killed because one of the barracks had not been ready in the required time, though others say he was killed because too few workers were working or because prisoners were missing. I'd been sent to Plaszow with all my coworkers from the sawmill in the Krakow ghetto. It was bitterly cold when we arrived in the middle of the night, and we fell asleep on the bare floor without anything to cover us. In the morning, while it was still dark, I washed myself in the snow — the latrines were not ready for use yet — and we started to work, still in the dark. I was assigned to work with a group of prisoners, carrying lumber on our shoulders to construction sites, and was reminded of the slaves in ancient Egypt; every few metres there were Ukrainian SS with whips, beating us mercilessly if we dared slow down.

A few days later, we were passing a carpentry shop when the foreman there pointed at me and said, "I know him. He used to work in the sawmill in the ghetto. He is an expert in sharpening saws, and that's the kind of worker I need very badly in the shop." The next day I was transferred to the carpentry shop, where I worked for the rest of my time at the Plaszow camp. The job was good, I was doing what I knew, but like everyone else I was still living in constant fear. Every day somebody was shot, killed without reason.

On February 11, 1943, the leadership of Plaszow was assumed by another SS officer, Amon Leopold Göth, which was the start of a period of unimaginable terror. The camp was still being built and the number of Jewish inmates multiplied every day. A tyrant and a sadist, Göth began a killing spree in connection with the building of the camp, starting with the Jewish architect and engineer Diana Reiter, who was responsible for the construction of the barracks. Göth ordered her killed because one wall collapsed.

At one point, some of the construction was not completed on time, prompting an announcement over the loudspeaker: "Everyone is to come to the Appellplatz." We assumed the standard formation, rows of five, while Göth selected a number of men and women, quite at random. The people who had been selected were beaten mercilessly. Midway through the beatings, one of the victims defecated. Göth walked straight to him and shot him in the back of the head.

One day when we were lined up on the *Appellplatz*, Commandant Göth singled out a man from the line and shot him through the head for no apparent reason at all. Göth then turned to the next person and asked, "Why are you staring at me so stupidly?" And he shot him as well.

When we saw Göth riding into the camp on his white horse, wearing his white gloves, we knew he would shoot at least a few people.

One time he came riding in followed by the two vicious dogs he always had with him, and he pointed two prisoners out to the dogs and just said, "Jews!" In a matter of minutes, those dogs had torn the prisoners apart. It happened right in front of our shop.

Seeing this, I came to the decision that if someone tried to harm me, I would fight back. I was working with saws and all kinds of cutting devices, so I had the opportunity to make a very sharp knife, which I then carried in my sleeve at all times. I made myself a promise: I would throw the knife first, before I was killed. One for one. I never had the opportunity to test whether I could do it.

Next to me in the barracks, there was a boy about my age whom I'd known before the war; we had belonged to the same scout group. I came back from work one day and found him lying face down with his buttocks bigger than the rest of his body, swollen and covered in blood. He told me he'd been working with some other people outside the camp and they'd discovered they were able to smuggle some food back, but that day they'd been caught. Göth and his henchmen had been waiting for them near the gate. "Empty your pockets!" the commandant had yelled. Mostly bread fell on the ground. "To whom does it belong?!" No one answered. Göth pulled his gun from its holster and started shooting at random.

Finally, he got tired of shooting and gave an order for everyone in the group to be whipped one hundred times, with the prisoners counting their own lashes aloud. If anyone made a mistake counting, their whipping would start again from the beginning, and in the morning they'd still have to show up to work. Many people died while being whipped, but the boy had miraculously survived. His name was Max Szyf, and he was one of my friends until his death in July 2001.

For a few weeks we had nothing to eat but carrots. It seems Göth had gotten a deal on them, so we ate carrots for breakfast, lunch, supper. No bread, no soup, just carrots and more carrots. They're supposed to be good for the eyes, but what about the stomach? I was so hungry that when I heard a rumour that the Ukrainian SS were keeping potatoes in the ground near the watchtower, I decided I'd go there during the night to try to steal some, and that same night I went to investigate. Not far from the watchtower there was a barracks, and I hid myself underneath it in a spot where I could observe the tower and its searchlight. I counted the time it took the light to pass over the potato field — one hundred seconds, which meant I could allow myself fifteen seconds to get in, fifteen to get out and sixty to pick the potatoes, leaving ten seconds to spare. The next night, that's exactly what I did, but I was so scared I never did it again.

I had no way to cook the potatoes, so for the next few days I ate them raw. Then I became very sick. I was diagnosed with typhoid and immediately put in a so-called hospital, in a separate quarantine section with other infected people. I can hardly remember the next few days, I had such a high fever, but one morning I woke up to a big commotion. The prisoner in the next bed said, "Göth is on his way to the hospital! We are all going to be shot!" Within a minute, the commandant arrived, and Dr. Gross gave him a list of all the people infected with typhoid. But then the doctor approached my bed and said to his orderly, "He is well already. Give him some cloths and a broom and let him start cleaning the barracks."

I was the only one left alive. Everyone else was shot that same day. Why did he save only me? I have been asking myself this question my whole life, and continue to do so. There were other young people in that hospital barracks whom he could have saved the same way. As I mentioned, he was hanged after the war, after being found guilty of war crimes.

One day in February 1944, Göth came to our shop early in the morning. He was drunk already and started screaming that he was having a big party that night and we had to make him a big comfortable chair by the evening. And if he didn't get it, he said he was going to kill everybody in the shop. No matter how hard we worked, it was impossible to make the chair in so little time, and the next day he shipped us all to Auschwitz.

The Luck of Selection

February 20, 1944. It was exactly one month after my eighteenth birthday when we were sent from Plaszow to the train that would take us to Auschwitz. There were so many of us crammed into the cattle car that we had to stand. Our group from the carpentry shop was packed together in the same car, and the trip took approximately two days, although it's only about seventy kilometres from Krakow to Auschwitz. I don't remember if we received any food during the transport — probably not; and I really don't remember how or where we relieved ourselves.

When the doors of the cattle car finally opened, it was early in the morning and we were greeted by yelling, screaming SS men, kapos (prisoners who oversaw other prisoners) and dogs. "Schnell! Schnell! Raus, verfluchte Juden!" (Fast! Fast! Out, cursed Jews!) The dogs were snarling and barking continuously at us. We were dirty, smelly and too weak to move very quickly, so our new enforcers used whips to encourage us to walk faster. We walked about three kilometres to a camp, which we later found out was called Birkenau.

We assembled in front of the gate of the camp and waited, for what we didn't know. A friend who was standing next to me asked, "Do you think that this is the end?" He meant selection first, crematorium next.

We waited for quite a while before a tall SS man came out of the gate looking at a sheet of paper. After a minute he looked at us and yelled, "Are you all skilled workers?"

Naturally, we yelled back, "Jawohl!" (Yes!)

We had been officially shipped from Plaszow as a group, documented as having worked in the carpentry shop, so he presumed correctly that we were skilled workers, and our lives were saved, for the time being.

It was a bitterly cold February day, and since those Germans were very clean and very cruel people, they forced us to be deloused before entering the barracks. Outside the "baths," we were made to strip off all our clothing. We stood in the freezing cold, completely naked, for God knows how long, before being herded into the building where, to our great surprise, we had a hot shower. But moments after we got wet, we were thrown outside again, dripping and shivering without any clothes.

At the direction of the screaming guards, we ran to our designated barracks, Barracks 18, but were prevented from entering by the next person who would be in charge of us, a *Blockältester* (block elder, a prisoner who served as the barracks leader), who greeted us with whips and speeches about us dirty, lousy Jews. After a couple hours of this, we were given our striped uniforms, a place to sleep and a piece of bread with hot, watery soup. Did that soup ever taste good!

Finally, I thought we could sleep; no matter if I had to share my bunk, which was nothing more than a shelf, with a number of other people. But no. "Alle raus!" (Everybody out!) More screaming and yelling as we ran outside to be counted again, and again. Eventually, we were allowed to sleep.

The next morning — or was it still night — we were woken by more yelling and screaming: "Aufstehen! Bett machen!"(Get up! Make the bed!) My close friend, with whom I'd shared the bunk, asked, "What's going on?" We soon found out — *Appell*, roll call. We had to assemble in front of the barracks in one minute to be counted. Those who were late were beaten. It was bitterly cold, and God forbid we should move an inch; the kapos were just waiting to beat us, perhaps to death. We had to stay at attention for hours until, finally, we heard the order, "Mützen ab!" (Hats down!), and the SS man came to count heads. And again there were beatings if we didn't remove our hats fast enough, or if we moved or lifted our eyes. This went on twice a day, every day.

But it was on that first day that I learned to disconnect myself from the hell around me by switching my mind from reality to thinking about the beautiful world that still existed somewhere else — to the sunrise and sunset, the blue sky with small clouds floating around forming different patterns, birds singing, and swimming. I recalled, especially, the wonderful summer of 1939, which I'd spent at summer camp in the Tatra Mountains. After that, whenever I was beaten, which was often, I thought about all those wonderful things and never felt the beatings.

On our second day, the kapos did a selection in the barracks. They made us undress completely and parade in front of them. It appeared they had the power to decide if we were fit to work or to go to the crematorium, and some of my friends and I were marked as skin and bones, unfit to work. Those of us given this designation were moved to a basement, where we waited for a few hours, completely naked and very cold. Then, "Achtung!" (Attention!) Dr. Mengele arrived to make the final decision as to who would live and who would be gassed. He looked at his paperwork and then yelled, "Are you all skilled workers?"

Naturally, we answered "Jawohl, Herr Doktor!" (Yes, sir doctor!) We were very happy because again we were saved, for the time being.

When we returned to the barracks, we were tattooed on the left arm with a number and given striped clothes with the same number and the Star of David sewn on them. My number was 174131.

The next day we went to work at a large workshop, making products for the war. I was assigned to work with a Polish carpenter, who kept telling me, "Keep yourself busy, keep moving."

I asked what I should do, and when he didn't respond I made myself busy picking up pieces of wood from the floor, until I smelled food and knew that any minute we'd be getting something to eat. I was right! The soup came in, and I received my portion, which I ate in a second. Now I was really hungry. I looked around and saw that most of the Polish prisoners, including my carpenter, hadn't touched what I considered the "delicious" soup. Apparently, some of them were able to get food into the camp from their families and saw no reason to eat the soup. I asked my carpenter if I could have his soup, and he said, "You can have as many as you want." That day I ate seven portions.

The next day was a repetition of the first: I could hardly wait for the soup to arrive, and when it did I again ate many portions. But that night I woke up around midnight with a terrible stomach ache. I barely made it to the latrine, where I stayed for the rest of the night. What am I going to do? I asked myself. To be sick in Auschwitz was as good as being dead. I made it back to the barracks a few minutes before the *Appell*, but I knew I wouldn't survive standing outside for at least two hours in the cold without moving a muscle, waiting to be counted. If I went to the *Appell* and then to work, I'd never survive; on the other hand, if I went to the infirmary, I'd have a very small chance of survival. I chose the second option.

I made it to the so-called hospital, where the doctor asked what was wrong with me. I answered that I had a very bad case of diarrhea, at which point he shouted at his orderly, "Franek! Go with him to the toilet and check if he shits constantly." I passed the exam; I was shitting without stopping.

The doctor sent me to block 19, a block for convalescent prisoners and a place from which Dr. Mengele selected people to be used as human guinea pigs in his experiments, but on the way I received some encouraging words from the orderly: "You are very lucky that you're going there today, because the selection for the crematorium by Dr. Mengele happened yesterday, and the next one will be in seven days." Well, I had another seven days.

In block 19 there was one room where all the people with dysentery were taken, and I entered to find about thirty very sick people, but what a surprise — I had my own bunk. In each room there was a prisoner-doctor and a *Stubenälteste*, a prisoner who served as a room leader. My doctor, Dr. Katz, was a Jewish prisoner from Belgium who'd been born in Poland, and the leader was a Pole named Bolesław, an ex-school principal and very big Polish patriot and antisemite.

A few minutes after I settled into my bunk, Dr. Katz came and asked me something in Yiddish. At that time I couldn't understand a word, since my family had never spoken Yiddish at home, so I answered in Polish that I was very sorry but I didn't understand Yiddish, adding that my family had spoken only Polish. This seemed to anger him, but Bolesław became very interested in our conversation and asked, "You really don't speak Yiddish? How come?"

I explained again that at home we spoke only Polish, and told him my father had been an officer in the Polish army. Then I added that my family kept all the Jewish traditions, but we were really Polish patriots. (I don't know how much truth there was in that, but it sounded good.) He seemed very impressed and turned to the Jewish doctor, saying, "You see, this boy is Polish of Jewish religion. That's how all you Jewish people are supposed to be." Then he turned back to me and said, "We will make you strong and healthy."

That turned out to be a difficult task. Nothing would stay in my stomach, and day by day I became a skeleton no matter what Bolesław brought me to eat. I overheard him and the doctor discussing what kind of medicine would help me and how to get it as quickly as possible, because they knew there would be a selection for the crematorium in a few days, and I was for sure a candidate.

The next day, Bolesław showed something to Dr. Katz and said, "I got it!" It was opium, which was apparently the best medicine for dysentery. Later, I learned there was a Polish underground in Auschwitz that would get medication to help prisoners in need. The leader of this organization was a man named Józef Cyrankiewicz, who became the prime minister of Poland after the war. I think he was the one responsible for getting my medication.

A couple of days later, I was just starting to feel a bit better when I heard a big commotion; Dr. Mengele was on his way. Bolesław rushed to me saying, "Janek, get up fast and get dressed. Here is a broom. Start sweeping the floor." This was the same thing Dr. Gross had done for me in Plaszow. I could hardly stay on my feet, but I did my best to move around. Then I saw him — the Angel of Death. Over seventy years have passed since that day, but I still feel that fear when I talk about it. Mengele pointed his finger at almost every sick person in the room, which meant they were selected for the crematorium. I was saved by a miracle.

Later on, after the war, many people asked me, "How did you survive?" And I have to tell them it had nothing to do with my ability to survive; it was 100 per cent luck, or if you are a believer (which I am not sure I am), you would say that somebody up there was watching over me.

But why me?

In a few days there was yet another selection. New sick people had come into the infirmary, and most of them were sent to the crematorium. Bolesław saved my life over and over again. But it was becoming very dangerous, as my chart clearly showed that I'd been in the hospital for a few weeks; dangerous not only for me, but for Dr. Katz and Bolesław as well.

But I was already a bit stronger, and one morning Bolesław came and said, "Janek, we are going to discharge you today, as another selection is due soon. But in a couple of days you will go back to the dispensary, ask for a certain person, and he will send you back to us."

The next morning, I was discharged and found myself walking through the camp to the new barracks I'd been assigned to. I was back in hell. I saw prisoners walking like zombies. I smelled the stench from the crematoria, which were working at full capacity because it was at this time that Hungarian Jews were being transported to Auschwitz by the thousands.

In the barracks I was shown where I was to sleep, between two Roma. The piece of bread I received that night was immediately stolen — no food till the next morning. And what a morning.

"Appell!" It was still dark, a cool morning, and I was wearing only the *Pasiak*, the striped jacket and pants that prisoners wore. It was the first time I started to lose any hope of surviving. But I remembered what Bolesław had told me about returning to the hospital in a few days. Could I survive a few days? I told myself I wasn't going to wait; I'd return the next day.

The next morning, I went to the dispensary and asked for the person I'd been told to request. He knew about me and sent me back to block 19, where Bolesław was waiting for me. "We are going to keep you here for a few days as a sick person, and then after that I will recommend that the *Blockschreiber* (the block secretary, who in this case was a member of the underground) make you an orderly's helper." It was my lucky day. A few days later I was an orderly's helper. My job included washing the floor in the morning, cleaning up after the sick and helping them to the toilet. I was even shown how to take people's temperature and pulse and to enter this data on their chart.

On the days when there was a selection, which happened almost weekly, my job was to wash the floor near the entrance and watch for the arrival of Dr. Mengele. As soon as I saw him, I was to yell as loud as I could, "Achtung!" This gave the staff a few minutes to hide some of the *Muselmänner*, people who were near death from starvation and exhaustion. Until a few days previous, I was one of them.

When I got a little bit stronger, I went every morning with some other prisoners to the kitchen, located a few blocks from the hospital, to bring pots of what they called coffee. One day, one of the prisoners working in the kitchen pointed to a specific coffee pot and said, "Take this one." When we picked it up, it was impossible not to notice how heavy it was. At the hospital we found the usual coffee on the top, but the bottom was full of cooked potatoes. We were able to feed the whole block for a couple of days. This happened a few times before that prisoner disappeared. I haven't the slightest idea what happened to him. I never spoke to him, but to me he remains an unnamed hero.

In October 1944, one of the crematoria was blown up! The great news was all around the camp — finally we'd scored a point against the Germans. We learned that a few young Jewish women working in the munitions factories had smuggled some explosives to prisoners working in the crematorium, and this squad of prisoners forced to work in the crematoria, called the *Sonderkommando*, blew it up in an attempt to slow down the killing. But our celebration was short-lived. The girls were caught and hanged in the *Appellplatz* in early January 1945, with the whole camp assembled to watch.

A few days later Bolesław disappeared; he was probably killed.

In the last few days before the evacuation of Auschwitz, the warehouses where the Germans kept the clothing, shoes and other items taken from those who had been transported to Auschwitz — we called the warehouses Kanada — were left completely unguarded. Two days before our evacuation, we went to the warehouses and helped ourselves to the best shoes we could find, warm coats, good woollen blankets — referred to as a Kanada blanket — and knapsacks, because we guessed we were about to be on the road for quite a while.

Staying Alive

In mid-January 1945, our section of Auschwitz was evacuated. The crematoria had stopped working two months earlier, since the Germans were busy covering their tracks. I was still working in the hospital on the day of the evacuation and could have stayed there with the sick people and waited to be liberated by the Soviet army, but I knew what would happen there — the Germans would kill everybody, as they always did.

I don't think I can describe the horrors, starvation, beatings and suffering of the next four months. A large crowd, perhaps three thousand, was gathered in front of the camp waiting for the order to leave. In total, the Germans forced almost sixty thousand prisoners to march west out of Auschwitz and its subcamps. While I was waiting, I found people from my transport from Krakow, and we promised we would help each other.

Once we were on our way, we walked as a group. We held on to each other. Time went so slowly, but we kept each others' minds occupied to avoid facing the uncertainty of what was to come. We knew our final destination was another camp, but we hoped something would hold us up along the way.

We walked through the night in the extreme cold, past many dead bodies. If anyone stopped, they were shot on the spot. My group from Krakow was very lucky; we stuck together and strengthened each other.

The next night we stopped at some kind of large farm, where the only place I could sleep was outside on the frozen ground. Somehow, the others had found a place in the barns, and in the morning I couldn't find them. Most likely they'd left before me.

We walked for days on end until we reached a train station in the town of Racibórz, Poland. The half of us who were still alive were put into an open train, like cattle. Time was a haze. The train crossed the Czechoslovak border, and when we arrived at the first town, Moravská Ostrava, the whole population was waiting for us with bread and hot soup. They fought the SS just to get close enough to us to give us some food. You cannot imagine what it's like when people are starving. Growing up, I was always taught to share, but in this situation everyone was fighting over small pieces of food. I got hold of a piece of bread, which I swallowed immediately. I'll never forget those courageous townspeople for as long as I live.

I had lost a lot of strength on that journey, but I knew if I gave up it would be over for me. I forced myself to keep going despite the starvation and the atrocities I saw along the way.

We arrived at Mauthausen on January 25, 1945, after a long journey in cold temperatures with barely any food, and I looked around for my friends from Krakow. Finally, I saw one standing in a daze, also looking about for somebody he knew. It was good to see him, and we promised we would try to stick together. It was easier to survive when you had a friend.

We stood in the freezing temperatures alongside thousands of others, all of us waiting our turn to take a bath. Only a small number of people were allowed in the showers at a time, which meant many waited, starving, in the frigid air for so long that they froze to death. I told my newfound friend that we had to get to the baths that day. We forced ourselves through the crowd and somehow got in. What a pleasant surprise! A hot shower! Although I no longer remember his name, without this friend I'd never have had the courage to push my way through that line.

At the baths we'd had to give up all of our clothing, but we were allowed to keep our shoes, and I was happy to keep mine, as they were very good ones I'd gotten from Kanada in Auschwitz. Afterward, we joined the others who'd already showered and waited, naked, until there were enough of us to fill a barracks. With the cold temperatures and wind, death was very near, and I was very thankful to have those shoes on.

When we arrived at our barracks, the *Blockälteste* — who in this case was a German criminal — gave us a long speech about the rules of the camp. I thought I was going to freeze to death, as we still had no clothes, but, finally, he finished speaking and gave us some clothing — rags — to get dressed in. When I think about it, I realize I didn't change those clothes until I was liberated more than three months later. We weren't given any socks, so we used whatever scraps of newspaper we could find to line our shoes.

We were given a small amount of food to eat, and I found a place to sleep that was safe from the overcrowding of all the others nearby. I slept on the floor of the barracks for a few days until we were taken to the Mauthausen railway station and sent on a short, three-hour journey to KL (*Konzentrationslager*) Melk.

We arrived at the Melk train station late in the afternoon and had to walk through the town to get to the camp. For me, it was an experience beyond comprehension. Here we were, going through a beautiful town, with lights in the windows through which I could see families sitting around their tables eating supper, children playing. I had completely forgotten something like this still existed. No one was on the street, but I saw people looking out their windows, pointing at us.

Shoes were the major commodity in the camp, and from the minute I arrived, it seemed as though every prisoner there was looking at mine, trying to figure out how to steal them. I was still wearing those leather shoes from Auschwitz while everybody else had roughly made wooden shoes. Most of the people at KL Melk were Soviet prisoners of war, and I was very lucky that one of them approached me and said, "I am an officer in the Soviet army, and my duty is to tell you that you better sell me your shoes because the others will steal them from you for sure and might even hurt you in doing so. I will give you three cigarettes, which you can exchange for bread, and my wooden shoes, which are about your size. If you don't want to do it, at least tie the shoes up to your neck when you go to sleep."

That night I was woken up a few times by people trying to pull the shoes from my neck, and I had to chase them away. First thing in the morning, I found the Soviet officer and made the trade.

The whole camp was engaged in building underground factories, completely bombproof, in the nearby mountains. The work was done only at night, under the cover of darkness, because during the day the Allies were bombing the German factories.

The next day, or rather night, we went to work in the mountains. We arrived after a short ride by train, and I was given a huge pneumatic drill by the kapo. The machine was bigger than me, but I was told to start drilling the rock out of the mountain. I couldn't even lift that drill. The kapo started yelling and beating me, but no matter how hard I tried I still could not lift the thing. I thought he was going to beat me to death, but I didn't feel the beating. The minute he started, I disconnected myself from what was happening, and in my mind I was back in a large open field with birds singing and white clouds floating in a blue sky.

All of a sudden, the kapo stopped beating me and said, "Take the wheelbarrow, shovel in the earth and dump it outside." I obliged him immediately. It was difficult, but much better than working in the tunnels with that drill.

To empty the wheelbarrow, I had to pass under a few watchtowers with their lights fixed on me. At one point while I was passing one of the towers I saw something fall into my wheelbarrow. I didn't dare look up, but when I emptied the wheelbarrow I found a large piece of bread. I couldn't believe my eyes. How was it possible that a German guard had taken pity on me and given me a piece of bread? But it happened, and not only once. Several nights when I was passing by around the same time, a piece of bread fell into my wheelbarrow.

I was at KL Melk for only a few weeks before I was shipped to another camp, Gusen, on March 17, 1945.

By now I had already experienced many camps, but nothing was like Gusen. There was practically no food. Once a day we received a bit of watery soup, if we were lucky enough to get it, and some mouldy bread. We had to line up for the bread, and every tenth person was given a loaf, which he was supposed to divide equally and share with the other nine. The first evening, the tenth person in the line was a Soviet prisoner, and as soon as he received the bread, the lights went out in the barracks and he simply disappeared. Nine of us didn't have anything to eat until the next evening, when I was very careful not to have a repetition of the previous night. We had to be very cautious even while eating the small piece of bread, because somebody might grab it from your hand and swallow it themselves.

Nights were the worst. The shelves we slept on were stacked three high, and we were lying next to each other like packed sardines. If we had to relieve ourselves during the night, we had to jump down from the bunk, run outside to the latrine and run back. As our food consisted mostly of liquids, we often had to pee at night. Sometimes it was impossible for people to control their bladder, and many people started peeing in the barracks, but there were a few kapos, mostly Roma, watching for this through the night, and if they caught you, they beat you to death.

At Gusen, we worked in nearby factories where the famous V-2 rockets were to be built, but not much work was being done because most of the time the factories were being bombed by the Allies. As soon as a train left with a rocket shipment, it was immediately destroyed by bombs, as were the incoming parts shipments. The airplanes sometimes completely covered the sky, and watching them became my favourite thing. It gave us hope that the end of the war was near.

That there wasn't much to do at the factory was a problem, though. There were no parts to work with, but we had to be constantly busy and moving quickly. If the kapo caught us doing nothing, he would beat us to death. Sometimes I installed one metal plate for the whole day; installing it and taking it out, installing, taking out.

By that time, I was skeletal. We weren't even getting the watery soup most days, because there were often air raids at mealtime. I had a constant buzzing in my ears and I was getting very weak. The only thing I could think of was food. But when I was beaten by the kapo, I didn't feel a thing because I disconnected myself completely from reality and dreamed about the blue sky, lakes with boats floating on them, and having a whole loaf of bread, cutting it slowly and eating it.

On April 2, 1945, we were sent back to Mauthausen.

On the way to Mauthausen from Gusen, a young man about two years older than me, around twenty years old, approached me and said, "My name is Joseph, and we should stay together and help each other. This way we will have a better chance to survive." I was more than happy to agree. At least I would have somebody to talk to and plan how to stay alive. Actually, Joseph was the one who did all the planning. I had found a new friend!

In March of 1945, thousands of Hungarian Jews had been forced to walk to Mauthausen. The barracks were full at that point, so tents were put up to accommodate them. Those who couldn't find room inside slept outside on the ground. At least they still had blankets, and some even had quilts that they'd brought with them from home. The Hungarian Jews had not been sent to the camps until the summer of 1944, because Hungary had been allied with Germany earlier, and the Hungarian Jews had been relatively well treated until the German occupation.

When we arrived back at Mauthausen at the beginning of April, it was still very cold, and we had no blankets or coats, since everything had been taken from us before we left Gusen — even our pots and spoons, which we soon learned were required if we were to get anything to eat.

The conditions in the camp were even more horrific now than they had been. There were dead bodies everywhere, piles of corpses lying right in front of the tents. We knew we had to try to get a place to sleep in one of the tents, but it was impossible; people were already lying inside, packed one on top of the other. We resigned ourselves to the fact that we would be sleeping outside, but the ground was still frozen, and without a blanket we would for sure freeze to death.

"Janek, we have to organize a couple of blankets and a pot so we can have some soup," Joseph said. I don't know how, but Joseph managed to "organize," the term used for trading and smuggling needed items, both things, and that night we sat on frozen ground, covered with the blankets, and ate some watery soup.

Like Ghosts on the Move

After a couple of weeks back in Mauthausen, we were again made to march, this time to Gunskirchen, about fifty-five kilometres from Mauthausen. This walk was truly hell on earth. More people died on this march than actually arrived at the final destination. Because the Hungarians had had better conditions for so long, they were not used to this experience, but I considered myself an old-timer, having survived for so long being hungry.

We spent the first night on an island in the Danube River. Watching the Hungarian prisoners, we learned from them that certain types of weeds could be eaten, as well as snails, which were plentiful on the island. I found out after the war that snails are a delicacy, eaten in expensive restaurants. But many people on the march died eating poisonous weeds.

The local population in areas we passed through didn't do much to help us. Some of us would often just run into houses to grab whatever was in the kitchen. Many were shot to death doing this. At that point I didn't care; I was so hungry I'd run into a house and grab whatever was cooking on the stove. The hunger was becoming unbearable. The locals were all afraid of us because we looked like ghosts, skeletons in rags. A few weeks later, the same population claimed they hadn't seen anything and they didn't know about any atrocities.

A few days later we arrived at KL Gunskirchen. The camp was

built in the woods near the village of Gunskirchen, around ten kilometres from a town called Wels. As we approached, we saw woods on one side of the road and the village on the other, but the second we got near the woods we smelled the dead bodies. At this point, there were very few Nazis left in the area. Everyone around me was dying of hunger and corpses surrounded us.

The first night we slept in one of the barracks. We had to sit between each other's legs, packed in tightly. As soon as it got dark and we started drifting off into semi-sleep, subconsciously we wanted to stretch our legs, but we couldn't because somebody was sitting between them, and our backs were pressed against somebody else. Consequently, the weak were pushed up and tossed like balls. At my back was Joseph, who was holding me tight to be sure I wouldn't be pushed up and thrown about. In the complete darkness, we could hear crying and screaming from those people who were being tossed around. Many of them were dead in the morning; they were just too weak, and this treatment killed them.

That was the longest night in my memory. Even now, more than seventy years later, I still have dreams of that night.

In the morning, some of the stronger people tied themselves with belts to the rafters inside the barracks, but Joseph announced, "We are not going to spend another night like this, no matter what. We will sleep outside." And finally we were able to get out. It was drizzling a bit, making the ground wet and muddy, but it was better than being inside. We found a couple of blankets and made a kind of tent. All around us, people, or I should say living skeletons, were walking aimlessly looking for some kind of food, which was nowhere to be found. A person I knew from Krakow was trading a piece of bread for a cigarette. I asked him why he would do that, and he replied that he was going to be dead soon, so he wanted to have a last cigarette. A few hours later we found him lying dead in the mud.

Freedom!

The morning of May 4, I was lying in our "tent," too weak to move, when I heard Joseph scream, "Janek! Get up, there aren't any guards! I went to the kitchen, where the guards usually were, but nobody was there. I was able to organize some potato skins, so let's run away and we'll cook them in the woods. We'll eat them like free men."

We were free!

Joseph showed me that he'd stolen a big knife, which he'd tied to the end of a stick, so we not only had potato skins to eat but also a weapon to defend ourselves. We were out of the camp, walking freely through the woods. We'd left the stink of the camp behind us, and we were breathing the beautiful aroma of pine trees. It was a gorgeous May day, and I could hear the birds singing, like they were happy for us. It was so hard to believe, but against all the odds, we were free. No more beatings, killings or starvation.

We'd been walking for about half an hour when we came across a small wooden house. We knew someone was there because there was smoke coming from the chimney, so we approached very slowly, knocked on the door and called out, "We are prisoners of war and we would like to have something to eat!"

The door opened slowly and, amazingly, a whole loaf of bread was pushed out. We devoured it in a few seconds, deciding to save the potato skins for later.

At the edge of the woods was a road leading to the town of Wels, and across the road was the village of Gunskirchen. As we were about to emerge from the forest onto the road, we heard boots marching and voices speaking in some foreign language that sounded like Dutch, which to us sounded like a mixture of English and German. "Let's hide," we whispered. "It must be the Dutch SS. If they see us, for sure we will be shot."

As we hid silently and continued to listen, I suddenly realized the language the soldiers were speaking was English. They were Americans! I leapt up, screaming, "We are free! We are free!" Joseph and I ran from the forest toward the soldiers — two young men looking more like ghosts, dressed in filthy rags, heads shaven, yelling in Polish, "We are Polish prisoners of war. There are thousands like us in the forest, dying by the hundreds every minute." I think we were afraid to say we were Jewish.

One of the soldiers approached us, and I still remember the horror in his eyes. He asked us something we couldn't understand. "Polish, Polish," we kept saying. There was one soldier who spoke Polish, and we told him about the camp in the woods. He immediately gave us some food and took us to a kind of dormitory in Gunskirchen, where we slept that first night of freedom on an army cot, which to us was like a king's bed. That day I learned my first English words, "I am hungry," which I repeated to every American soldier I saw.

It's hard to describe the feeling of waking up the next morning in freedom — no more starvation, no more guards, no more beatings, no more killings. We were really free!

Joseph and I decided we should go to the nearest town, Wels. We were still wearing the rags from the camp, full of lice, but after washing ourselves the best we could, we set out. There was hardly anybody from the local population on the road. I guess they'd locked themselves behind their doors, fearing retaliation. And the ones we met on the road were very lucky we were too weak to do anything when they all had the same thing to say: "My God, we didn't know anything!" How was it possible they didn't know what was happening when, only two weeks earlier, we living skeletons had been marched through their villages, desperately stealing food from their kitchens, being beaten or shot in front of their homes. They had witnessed the atrocities!

It was already getting dark when my friend and I reached the outskirts of the town. We knocked on several doors asking for a place to sleep for only one night, but nobody answered. Just as we were resigning ourselves to sleeping outside, a door opened, and the good people in the house let us in, gave us a home-cooked supper and let us sleep on their floor. It had been three years since I'd been in a real home, spoken to regular people and eaten at a table with a knife and fork. A couple of months later, we visited them and brought them a present, which they didn't want to take. We were lucky to have found some good people.

The next day we could hardly walk. Both of us felt very sick and realized we needed to get to a hospital. Following the directions we were given, we finally arrived at a hospital run by the Sisters of Mercy. We were not the first survivors to arrive there. The nuns, in their black habits, cried as they undressed us, seeing humans who were only bones and skin. They helped us take our first bath in months and then they weighed us. I weighed thirty-five kilograms — seventy-seven pounds. They dressed me in clean clothes and put me in a clean bed, which I didn't have to share with anybody.

I can hardly remember the next few weeks. I was horribly sick with typhoid fever. Most of the time I was delirious, running a very high temperature. The only thing I remember is refusing to let the German doctors near me, yelling at them that they were the murderers from the camps and that instead of helping me, they were going to kill me. Finally, they brought in an American doctor, who was able to put my mind at ease.

During my fever and hospital stay, I was separated from my friend Joseph and I never saw him again.

When I finally got well, I was transferred to a Displaced Persons (DP) camp near the town of Wels. I found it hard to believe that after all the suffering, I was again living in a barracks. A DP camp hardly compares to Nazi concentration camps, but still, I was not completely free, since I had to share one small space in my barracks with several other people. At least we were free to walk around the town, which I did every day.

And I found myself a job! Walking through town one day, I came across a place where American soldiers were stationed, and I went inside to tell them I'd gladly work for food. They said they needed somebody to wash dishes, and because I was going to be working in the kitchen, there would be plenty of food.

On my first day of work, I scraped any food left on plates into an empty tin and took it back to the camp. I gave it to my newfound friend, Joe Hefter, who really had a feast. He was very weak and thin, just recovering from typhoid fever, and he appreciated that food so much.

A few days later, while I was filling the empty tins with the leftover food, I realized the cook, an American soldier, was watching me. He came over and said, "What are you doing with this shit?"

I said, "This is not shit; this is good food, which I bring back to the DP camp. There are many people there who are waiting for it."

He didn't respond, but when I finished my work that night he was waiting for me in the Jeep and told me to get in, that he would give me a lift to the DP camp. When I jumped in and looked in the back seat, I couldn't believe my eyes — the whole seat was full of canned foods, oranges, bananas, so much food. He looked at me and started laughing. "I emptied the kitchen completely! The only thing I left there are hot dogs. There will be no more scraping the plates, and I will make sure you guys have enough food."

It's hard to describe people's excitement when we brought all that food into the barracks that night. The soldier divided it among everyone, and I could see that he almost cried when people thanked him for his kindness. He did this a few more times, but after some weeks he was gone, transferred to another division. I guess the soldiers had had enough of eating hot dogs every day.

∼

Thirty years later, when I was living in Canada, my wife, Sally, and I decided we were going to buy a condo in Florida. It was in a gated community in Deerfield Beach, and to be accepted to live there we had to talk to the sales manager. The man looked very familiar to me, but I couldn't place him. He asked all kinds of questions and we somehow started to talk about my experience right after the war. I told him about the work I'd done washing dishes for the US army. He looked at me in a strange way and asked where this had happened. I said it was in Austria, in the town of Wels. All of sudden he started to cry and said, "Remember me? I am the cook who brought the food to the camp!"

Later that day we had a celebration. He called all the salespeople to his office and sent for a bottle of champagne; it almost felt like he was declaring a national holiday.

Building a Home in a Camp

In October 1946, we were transferred to a beautiful apartment complex in Bindermichl, a suburb of Linz, Austria. Linz is one of the largest cities in Austria, located on the banks of the Danube River. In 1945, it was divided between the Americans and the Soviets, with the Americans on one side of the river and Soviets on the other. In the suburb of Bindermichl, there was a relatively new development of three-storey apartment buildings, each apartment having three bedrooms, a full-size kitchen and a complete bathroom. Part of this development was requisitioned by the American authorities and given to Jewish survivors.

It was basically a DP camp run by the people living there. We had our own mayor, police, clinics and schools. Each apartment had two small bedrooms and one large one. In our apartment, I shared the large bedroom with my friend Joe Hefter. Joe was a few years older than me, with much more experience in life, and I learned a lot from him. We bought ourselves a radio, and he showed me how to dance. We had plenty of opportunity to practise, as almost every day there was a wedding in the camp community, and everyone was invited. In the centre of the camp there was a reception hall, where we had dances every Saturday with the Spielberg Brothers, an excellent orchestra. We also had Jewish theatre, performed by some Jewish actors, most of whom were from the Soviet Union.

We had a very good soccer team, too — Hako'ach — which competed with Austrian teams. The captain of the team, Adam Elbaum, had been a good friend of my late brother Romek. Every time there was a home game between Hako'ach and an Austrian team, the whole camp was there, cheering our boys.

Food was still scarce, as everything was rationed except bread and mustard, but once in a while we got Red Cross packages, which helped us a great deal.

One of my neighbours was Simon Wiesenthal. He was in his mid-thirties, a good-looking man with a small moustache, always writing articles and letters to the editor of the local newspaper, mostly in response to antisemitic articles written by Nazis and Nazi supporters. He was our spokesman. He brought hundreds of pictures of accused Nazis into the camp, searching for witnesses to their crimes, and he found plenty in the community. Later, he became one of the best Nazi hunters in the world, and he is credited with many convictions of Nazi war criminals.

Through the Red Cross, I found an uncle who'd been living in Switzerland since long before the war. I wrote him a letter telling him who I was and describing the situation I found myself in. A couple of weeks later, I received a reply — I had never been so hurt and insulted. He wrote that he had an Austrian friend who told him that we DPs had everything, even more than the Austrians, and that we were all black marketeers. Near the end of the letter he asked if I had a profession and if I was going to school.

I replied, giving him a piece of my mind. I don't remember exactly what I wrote, but I guess he started to find out what had really happened to us, and a few weeks later a package arrived from him with a letter informing me that an American woman was coming to Linz to organize an ORT school (Organization through Rehabilitation and Training), and that she would come to see me. Apparently, this uncle was a big *macher*, an influential person, in the ORT organization. I smelled the Swiss chocolate in his package, but I sent it back to him without opening it.

The American woman's name was Sylvia Margulies. She was a tall, good-looking lady in her early forties, who located me in Bindermichl and came to our apartment. When I opened the door, she gave me a hug and kisses on both cheeks, and I was embarrassed by the show of affection, not knowing if I should kiss her as well, so I just shook her hand and introduced myself. We talked for a while. She said that she had spoken with my uncle in Switzerland and he was very sorry about the letter. She told me that she had, in fact, come to organize the ORT school.

The ORT school was opened in Bindermichl in September 1947, and together with some other boys, who are still my good friends today, I enrolled to study electronics. In no time at all, we'd covered the entire high school curriculum — subjects ranging from physics and mathematics to chemistry and drawing. We were trying to make up for lost time. We had excellent teachers for every subject, but our instructor for electronics and physics was especially good. His name was Maik, and he was not much older than us, but he always said, "As long as I know one more lesson than you, that's all it takes."

One of my good friends from the school was Joe Luden, a fellow a little older than me. During the war he'd been in the Soviet Union, where he'd joined the Polish army and had become an officer by the time he was eighteen. He was a very tough young man. Once we were on a streetcar full of Austrians, and as we passed our DP camp one of them said to another, "Do you know that those Jews have everything — food, money, clothing — and we have nothing."

Without a second of hesitation, Joe hit him in the face, yelling, "You bloody Nazi, how dare you talk like that!" There were about fifty Austrians on that car and only two of us. They could easily have beaten us to death, but they were completely quiet. The driver stopped the streetcar immediately and begged us to get out. We did just that.

My friend and roommate, Joe Hefter, married a very nice girl and soon after immigrated to Winnipeg, Canada, where they had some relatives who sponsored them. Everybody in the camp was looking for a way to immigrate to the US, Canada, Australia, South America or anywhere else, so they could leave the awful memories of the past behind and start a new life.

In early 1948, a representative from the Canadian Jewish Congress came to Linz to register and help Jewish orphans immigrate to Canada. Joe Luden and I found out about it and immediately put our names down. Canada! When I was in the concentration camps, we called all the best items Canadian: We called the best blankets "Canadian" blankets, working in "Canada" was what we called the best job, and on and on. My dream was that if I survived, I would be lucky enough to go to the best country in the world, Canada.

Canada and the Road to Happiness

Finally, in August 1948, we received our visas and started to make preparations for departure. I was the happiest person in the world. It was the beginning of a new life.

On August 12, 1948, I left the DP camp in Linz, Austria. We were a large group of war orphans under the sponsorship of the Canadian Jewish Congress (CJC) and the watchful eye of Mr. Reimer, who had been sent by the CJC to assist us right through our journey. Our whole class came to the railway station to say goodbye, and we were finally on our way. My dream was coming true.

A few days later, we arrived in Hamburg, Germany, where we waited for the ship that would carry us to Canada. That group of orphans became my family. We were all teenagers, the youngest being thirteen years old and the oldest not more than eighteen. Yes, I was really twenty-two, but to be able to immigrate, I changed my name to Ephroim Jablon and gave my birthdate as July 31, 1931.

We were so young but at the same time very mature. We ate together, sang together, played together, took walks together — like one big family. All these years later, some of those kids are still my best friends.

Finally, our ship arrived, and on September 18, 1948, we left Germany. I promised myself I would never go back there.

The ship was the *General Langfitt*, a very old military transport.

But who cared? We were the happiest bunch of kids in the world. The fun started after we'd crossed the English Channel and arrived on the open Atlantic, after the first day when everybody was seasick. A sailor took pity on us, brought us oranges and took us on deck for fresh air. He said, "Sing, walk, be busy, but do not sit inside. You will be okay." We took his advice, and for a couple of days we had a ball, exploring the ship, drawing pictures, eating well. But the following day, we noticed sailors installing ropes all around the ship. My friend Joe asked mockingly, "What is going on? Are you expecting a hurricane?"

The sailor got very mad. "Don't ever say the word *hurricane* again. Yes, we are expecting a storm, so be very careful when you are on the deck."

Within a few hours it began; the sky got very dark and the sea became extremely rough. The ship was bouncing up and down like a toy. One second, we would see nothing but the angry sea, and the next moment only the bow of the boat was visible. The first few minutes were fun, but it soon got very scary. One after the other, we became seasick again and had to run inside, where it was much worse than being on the deck. The first to get ill was Bumi Leibovitch. He was so sick that we had to take him to the infirmary, where he kept moaning, "Canada no good." The rest of us decided we were going to stay on deck as long as possible.

The storm lasted for hours, but the next morning the sun came out and the weather was beautiful. We watched a school of dolphins follow the ship for quite a while, and we learned the weather had turned for the better because we were approaching the Gulf Stream.

On October 1, 1948, we arrived at Pier 21 in Halifax, Nova Scotia, Canada. My dream had come true. "I am in Canada!"

Well, not yet. First I had to go through an immigration process, where I was asked many, many questions, and then I remember the officer asking me, "Why did you come to Canada?"

Without thinking twice, I answered, "Because this is the best country in the world." He gave me a strange look, and that was the end of his questions. The next moment I walked through the gate and I was really in Canada.

Mr. Reimer, the representative from the Canadian Jewish Congress, was waiting for us on the other side and continued to be our guide and adviser for some time into our lives in Canada, but on that Halifax pier we had so many questions for him: "How are we going to our destination?" "Where are we going to get some food?"

He had a little smile on his face as he said, "Please stop worrying, because everything is taken care of." And he was right.

We boarded the luxury train that would take us to Montreal. I could not believe my eyes; it was a sleeper. My friend Joe Luden and I had two whole seats to ourselves, and at night, the porter came and made them into beds. But before we went to bed, we were served food in the dining room. What a life!

All day and most of the night, I looked through the window, watching the big country unfold before my eyes, and the next morning we arrived in Montreal. Some kids from our group went on to Toronto and Winnipeg, but for us, Montreal was to be home.

Trains enter Montreal's CN rail station underground, so when we arrived it took quite a few minutes to get out and actually see the city, but what a beautiful sight it was. The first thing I saw was the Sun Life Building, a very tall and grand building, the largest building by square footage in the British Empire when it was built. Hundreds of cars and hundreds of peoples moved in every direction. I could see the city vibrating with life and knew I had made the right decision choosing Montreal as the place to start my own new life.

We boarded buses that were waiting for us near the train station and took a short ride to the Herzl Health Centre, originally called the Herzl Hospital and Dispensary, located on Jeanne Mance Street, at the corner of Mount Royal Avenue. The Herzl Health Centre was adapted to accommodate the influx of orphaned Holocaust survivors. It could house a total of fifty people in a few large rooms, and also had a reception room, kitchen and dining room downstairs.

When we arrived at the centre, we were greeted by quite a few people who'd all come to see us, most likely with the intention of adopting some of us. They were a bit disappointed, as some of them had been expecting young children, rather than "old" teenagers like us (I was really in my twenties, after all). But those people were wonderful, and the next morning some of them came with their cars to show us around the city.

Mr. Reimer continued as our counsellor and guide and was the person who introduced us to the activities of Jewish life in Montreal. Right around the corner from the centre, on Mount Royal Avenue between Jeanne Mance and Park Avenue, was the YMHA. Next to it was the famous Dunn's delicatessen, where, at that time, a smoked meat sandwich cost fifty-five cents. I couldn't afford to go there for a while, but it was the gathering place after movies. Not far from us, on Esplanade Street, was the Jewish Public Library, where the famous Jewish writer Melech Ravitch gave a lecture once a week. And I shouldn't forget the beautiful Mount Royal Park and Fletcher's Field, right around the corner (now called Jeanne-Mance Park).

It was at the centre that we kids formed very close relationships, like a family, so that, even now as I write my memoirs all these years later, we are still very close — Lina Koch, Charlotte Wolf and many others. Max Szyf, Joe Luden and Bumi Leibovitch are now all deceased.

We arrived at the centre just a few days before Rosh Hashanah, the Jewish New Year, and on the first night of the holidays, we were all invited to different homes. Joe Luden and I found ourselves at the home of the Gordon family in Outremont. We hadn't been very happy about the invitation, as we'd rather have spent the holiday with our friends at the centre, but as was explained to us, it's good to make connections. Looking back, those people were very kind to us, but we felt so strange there, completely out of place in their lovely home.

The next night, we decided to celebrate at the centre. We had a good supper, but an hour later a car arrived to take us to another family's home for dinner. We argued, "How can we go and have another supper?"

Someone who worked at the centre insisted that we accept this invitation and replied to me, "Well, this is a very important family in Montreal. So you better go. They came specially to pick you up." I didn't know who these people were, but even later when I found out they were one of the richest families in Montreal, I didn't really care.

The evening was a disaster. They lived in a gorgeous house on Côte-Sainte-Catherine Road, facing the mountain. Their table was beautifully set with a centrepiece of exotic flowers. The husband sat at the head of the table with his wife on one side of him and his son on the other. There was also a setting for their daughter, but apparently she didn't want to come down, we assumed because of us poor refugees.

The fun began when the husband said, as he carved the turkey, "In this country you eat with a fork and knife. You hold the fork in the right hand and the knife in the left."

Joe and I looked at each other, our expressions silently saying: What's wrong with this person? What does he think we are? Without thinking twice, Joe answered him sarcastically. "That's something new. We thought that we were supposed to eat with our fingers." I think he got the message.

We didn't touch our food, giving the excuse (Joe's idea) that we'd purchased some peanuts that afternoon and, having never had them before, we'd eaten so many that we both had a stomach ache.

When the supper was finally over, the man tried to give us some money, which we naturally refused, very politely. Looking back at that episode now, I'm sure they meant well, and I have to acknowledge that the people of Montreal's Jewish community, particularly the wealthy ones, were responsible for my being in Canada.

A few days later, everyone from the centre was sent to live with different families. I was chosen to live on Old Orchard Avenue in the Montreal neighbourhood Notre-Dame-de-Grâce (NDG), with relatives of the owners of the big Steinberg's supermarkets. Joe Luden was placed not far from me, while Charlotte Wolf was placed with an influential family in Westmount and Lina Koch, who was the youngest, was adopted by a very nice couple, Mr. and Mrs. Latanski, in Outremont.

I lasted one day on Old Orchard Avenue. Shortly after I arrived, the gentleman of the house showed me around their very nice home. It had a number of bedrooms upstairs, with a living room, dining room and kitchen downstairs, and even a finished playroom in the basement. Then he took me to the bathroom. "Here," he exclaimed, "is a bathroom! In this house, the water comes from the wall." I was speechless. What was he going to show me next? I asked myself. He then bent over the bathtub and turned on the water.

I immediately flipped the lever for the shower, saying, "And what is this?" Of course, water poured down all over the poor gentleman. I must say, he wasn't mad, but that was the end of the sightseeing. I don't know why he thought I'd never seen running water. Perhaps he'd come to Canada at the beginning of the century from a small village, where the only source of water was a well in the middle of the village. In any case, the next day I was back at the centre and promised myself I'd never be a charity guest again; I would find myself a job and pay my own way.

Lina was very lucky. She found wonderful people in the Latanskis. She stayed with them until she got married, when they gave her a beautiful wedding. But Joe's experience was similar to mine, and he also returned to the centre within a day. We immediately started looking for jobs and a place to live. The CJC assigned us a social worker, Miss Fisher, an understanding person who took care of our needs. When she heard about my adventure with the Steinberg relatives, she laughed and said, "Good for you." It was the first time I'd heard that expression.

Miss Fisher took us to Eaton's department store, where we purchased necessary things like underwear, socks and pajamas. Then she gave us vouchers to purchase a suit and a winter coat at Schreter's, a store on Saint Laurent Boulevard near Saint Catherine Street.

Joe and I looked around the store and found more or less what we wanted, but when we showed the suits to the owner, he got mad and shouted, "You're not supposed to choose from this section! There's where you're going to choose from." And he pointed to a different area of the store.

"Those rags, you can wear," said Joe.

The owner (or perhaps he was a salesperson) got so red in the face I was afraid he was going to have a stroke. He screamed, "Get out of the store and never come back!" Then he tried to physically throw Joe out.

Joe looked at him very coolly and said, "You just try to lay hands on me and you will be very sorry."

I think the man was afraid of Joe, because he just walked away without saying another word. Years later, Joe became a very successful sportswear manufacturer, and the Schreter's store was one of his best clients.

Back at the centre, Miss Fisher was waiting for us. She said she'd received a complaint from the Schreter store about our behaviour and wanted to hear our explanation. She listened to our story and didn't say a word. Later on, we had a long talk with her and explained that we didn't want to be a burden to the Jewish Congress or community anymore, that we wanted to get jobs, find a place to live and continue our education at night.

We were quite advanced in our education, since we already had diplomas in radio engineering from the ORT school in Linz and good knowledge of higher mathematics, physics, chemistry and some other subjects. By this time, our close friends from the ORT school in Austria, Dave Blitzer and Mayer Friedman, had arrived in Montreal and on the recommendation of Miss Fisher, we all went to register at Sir George Williams University (now Concordia University) for the next semester. Our plan was to get high school equivalency certificates by summer of the next year and continue into college programs in the fall, and we were accepted to the school without having to pay tuition for one full year.

In the meantime, the problem of where to live was solved. Joe's sister and her husband, Mr. and Mrs. Lanail, and their seven-year-old daughter, Mirele, immigrated to Canada. They rented a small apartment on Clark Street near Mount Royal Avenue, next to the ice factory, and they gave us one room for fifteen dollars a week each.

It was a very small, old apartment with two bedrooms, one of which I shared with Joe while Mr. and Mrs. Lanail and Mirele shared the other. There was only a tiny bathroom without a shower, just a bathtub that was always full of dirty laundry, so I was happy the YMHA was only a few blocks away, and I went there every night to swim and shower. In spite of the limited space and inconvenience, I was very happy in that apartment. The Lanails were like parents to me; they went out of their way to make me comfortable. Every morning, Mrs. Lanail asked me what I'd like for supper, and what kind of a cake I'd like. Mr. Lanail was well educated, played the violin and painted beautiful pictures. He also spoke perfect French and English, so he had no trouble finding a job.

The CJC paid our first two weeks' rent, so I had to find a job quickly, since in two weeks I had to start paying for my own room and board. Miss Fisher suggested I go to the Jewish Vocational Services (JVS), but they were not much help. I was trying to get a job in my field, in electronics, but there wasn't any work in that area, as it would still be a few years before it was common for people to have televisions in their homes. I was told to forget about electronics and get a job in the garment industry, where there was plenty of work.

"What do I know about the *shmatte* business?" I asked the person at JVS.

"Don't worry," they replied, "you will be trained to be a cutter and will make a good living."

JVS sent me to a place on Ontario Street, near Bleury. It was an old, dilapidated building without an elevator, and the factory, Monarch Garment, was on the third floor. As I walked in, I was struck by the noise, heat and lack of fresh air. In the front there was a small office area, where the receptionist asked me what I wanted. I said I'd been sent by Jewish Vocational Services to work, to which she looked me up and down and gave a yell into an intercom: "Benny, somebody to see you for a job!"

"Let him wait! I am busy now!" This blared through the intercom. I waited about fifteen minutes before Benny, who was apparently the boss, showed up. "So, you are the *greeneh* who wants to be a cutter?"

"I beg your pardon, my name is Johnny Jablon, not Green, and yes, I came here to get a job." I didn't know *greeneh* meant newcomer; I thought he'd made a mistake with my name, which I had Anglicized.

"The pay will be fourteen dollars a week, and if you work very hard, in a few weeks you will get a raise."

"Sir," I said very politely, "I have to pay fifteen dollars a week for my room and board and I will need some money for the bus, so for me fourteen dollars a week will be impossible to get along on."

"Okay, I will give you seventeen dollars and you can start work tomorrow. Do you have scissors?"

"No."

"Murray! Mr. Green is here for a job!" Later I learned Benny loved to insult people; it made him feel superior. Murray, the head cutter, came in, and I liked him immediately. He introduced himself and said, "Don't worry, I have an extra pair of scissors you can use until you can afford to buy your own."

The next day I walked to work, since I couldn't afford the bus. It took me about forty-five minutes, but I arrived before eight o'clock and had to wait a few minutes before the receptionist, who was also the bookkeeper, came in. She gave me my punch card and told me as I punched in that if I was even one minute late, she'd be obliged to take fifteen minutes out of my pay. I quickly calculated that would be about twenty cents, a bus ride one way.

The factory itself consisted of one large room with sewing machines, the finishing area, presses and the stockroom on one side, and the cutting room and shipping area on the other. To get material from the stockroom to the cutting table, I had to go right by the presses, and Murray warned me ahead of time that one of the pressers was a bully, who'd try to trip me when I passed close to him carrying the material. Murray said even Benny was afraid of him.

At exactly eight o'clock, the bell rang and the pandemonium started. The noise from the sewing machines combined with the steam hiss from the presses and, above all, the yelling from Benny were overwhelming. The only person who was completely calm was Murray. He showed me exactly what to do and told me to bring some material from the stockroom to be cut. "Watch for the bully," he reminded me.

And it happened. While I walked back from the stockroom fully loaded with material, the big presser — who was at least twice my size — tried to trip me. I didn't say a word, but I asked Murray to let me go to the stockroom again. He said okay, but don't do anything foolish. This time I took the big scissors with me, hidden behind the apron I was wearing. Sure enough, the presser tried to trip me again, but this time I was ready. I took out the scissors and said to him very calmly, "Listen very carefully, you big piece of shit. If you don't want to have your head split with these scissors, you better stop doing this."

He became speechless, then said under his breath something like, "Look at the greeneh."

At three o'clock the bell rang, and Murray told me I should take a fifteen-minute coffee break. To my surprise, the bully presser brought me coffee and a May West (a popular creme-filled cake), saying, "No hard feelings, eh?" And he never bothered me again.

Friday. Payday! I would receive the first money I'd earned myself in Canada. At five o'clock I received my pay envelope. When I opened it, there was eighteen dollars inside instead of the seventeen I'd agreed to. I didn't complain and decided to take the bus home. I went to the City and District Bank at the corner of Mount Royal Avenue and Saint Laurent Boulevard and opened a savings account with ten dollars. After that, I made sure that every Friday I deposited something into my account.

Saturday night was a movie night. My friends and I went to a double feature at the Regent Theatre on Park Avenue, paying thirty-five cents, and afterward we walked on Park, where we met lots of people taking advantage of the few nice days left in autumn.

As the days became shorter and colder, winter was fast approaching. We now had a large group of friends, and with the help of Mr. Reimer, we organized a club at the YMHA, where we spent most of our free time. Once in a while we had a guest speaker, a book review or other presentation, and our volleyball team was performing very well, competing with different teams all over the city. We were wonderfully busy.

Two nights a week, I attended classes at Sir George Williams with two close friends, Dave Blitzer and Mayer Friedman. We were still planning to get our high school equivalency in one year. Our main subjects were trigonometry, algebra, physics, chemistry, geometry and English, and we found everything very easy, except English. We had to write an essay on the Shakespeare play *The Merchant of Venice*. I read it once, and then again, and I was still not sure if the play was written in English. I asked our teacher this, and she burst into laughter.

"You know what," she said, "come to my house on the weekend and I will explain the play."

On Saturday we went to her place on Hutchison at the corner of Bernard, and she explained the whole play so simply, by showing it to us in a comic strip. I found the story very offensive and antisemitic, and I expressed my feelings in my essay. I got 60 per cent, which was just barely a passing mark, but I was very happy I hadn't failed. We passed the rest of our subjects with marks of 90 per cent or higher. I asked my math teacher why I got only 99 per cent in algebra. He said only the teacher gets 100 per cent. I thought that was a stupid answer.

It started to snow at the beginning of December and didn't let up for two weeks. I'd never seen so much snow in my life and I loved it. We were living on the ground floor and every morning we had to shovel the snow that almost completely covered the front door just to get out of the house. I got hold of some old skis and ski boots and on weekends I spent both days skiing on nearby Mount Royal.

In the weeks before Christmas, the city looked beautiful, especially Saint Catherine Street, downtown. The windows of the department stores were beautifully done up, and many evenings we took long walks just admiring the decorations. For me it was a wonderful novelty — my first winter far from war-ravaged Europe and the horrors of the concentration camps, free to experience joy.

As I mentioned, one of my friends, Lina Koch, was adopted by a very nice, childless, older couple, Mr. and Mrs. Latanski, and they treated her like their own. They lived in a large house on Davaar Avenue in Outremont and suggested that Lina invite her friends over for a party.

We organized everything. Each of us chipped in a dollar, which was the maximum we could afford, but it was enough to purchase a gallon of wine (three dollars), bread, salami, some decorations and, most importantly, a record of tangos, mambos and other dance songs. It was a terrific party — even now, having been to some fancy affairs, I still remember that party as the best.

Later in the evening, Mr. and Mrs. Latanski came downstairs, and we could see the joy on their faces as they watched us having such a good time. Mr. Latanski glanced at the bar and, seeing our wine and salami sandwiches, he went upstairs and returned in a little while with a big plate of smoked meat, smoked turkey and a bottle of Canadian Club. Without saying a word, he took the cheap wine away.

∼

Working as a cutter in the garment industry meant I had to belong to a union. In the summer, I learned that the owner of a hotel in Saint-Faustin-Lac-Carré, in the Laurentian mountains just north of Montreal, gave substantial discounts to union members. (He was a communist.) A group of us decided to go. It cost us thirty-five dollars each for a week at his hotel, including food and entertainment. We took a bus, and as the mountains came into view the whole world seemed to open up to me; it had been many years since I'd seen anything so beautiful. And the fresh air! These memories remind me of how much fun Canada has been.

The hotel was a dilapidated building. We all shared a five-by-ten-foot room with only two beds and a rack to hang our clothes. No toilet, no sinks, and the only shower for the entire floor was in the hall. In the morning, we had to line up to get to the shower, but none of us cared because we were so happy to be there. I couldn't wait each morning to get out and start the day. When we went to the dining room the first morning, the son of the owner told us we had to use a fork and knife — did he think we came from the jungle? But they served us beautiful food, including delicious oatmeal. There was always milk and cream on the table, and we all started putting cream on our cereal. We ate a lot of bread as well, asking for more as soon as each basket was empty, and saving some for later. The hotel owner lost lots of money on us because we ate so much. After breakfast, we all ran to the lake to get a boat. I was a very good swimmer and I bet my friends I could swim across while they took the boat. And I did. We played volleyball and soccer every afternoon, all afternoon. It was the best vacation ever — the time of my life.

Becoming a Family

In the summer of 1951, one of my good friends introduced me to a lovely young woman named Sally Pancer. We made a date, and from then on we saw each other every day. Sally was also from Poland, but during the war she had been taken to Siberia with her family and some friends. She was very young during the war, and she and her little sister went to school the entire time they were there, but her father was killed early in the war and it wasn't long before her mother was arrested for selling goods on the black market. Fortunately, one of the police officers who arrested her mother took care of Sally and her sister; he was like a father to them and treated them well. Their mother was eventually released, and after the war they returned to Poland and then were in a DP camp in Austria. Their mother remarried and had an opportunity to go to the US, but she could only bring one child. She took Sally's sister and left Sally at the DP camp by herself. We were actually in the same camp at the same time but didn't know it until years later when I discovered a picture with both of us in it. Sally became a nurse and eventually immigrated to Canada, but registered herself as a dressmaker rather than a nurse because she was told there was more demand for dressmakers here.

When we started seeing each other, Sally was working in a hat factory, I was still a cutter at Monarch Garment finishing my degree at night, and we were both paying for room and board, Sally at 226

Saint Viateur. At the end of each date, she insisted that we go Dutch (share the cost); I didn't want to, but she insisted. Every weekend we went dancing — she was very good — at Chez Parée or the Belvedere Theatre, or we enjoyed going to a movie. We got married on January 20, 1953, and lived in Sally's place until we got our own apartment at Bernard Street and Bloomfield Avenue. The apartment was like a palace to us.

Our daughter, Debbie, was born in 1957 and was immediately the apple of my eye.

∼

In 1952, I graduated from Sir George Williams University with a degree in electronics. Television was becoming very popular, so instead of going to work for a large company, like Marconi, I decided to open my own electronics sales and service business, with Sally supporting us as I developed my business. With my future partner, Alex Kurzman, I found a very small store on Queen Mary Road, near Circle, and we called our business Magic Touch TV Sales & Service.

From then on, the years went very quickly, and we grew from a small store to a very large one, always on Queen Mary Road. My only regret was not having much time to be with my family because I was so busy with the store, which just kept growing.

In 2000, after being in business for forty-eight years, I decided to retire.

I Found My Revenge

The day finally arrived. On April 10, 2018, at 9:00 a.m., a taxi brought me to the airport to meet the other survivors alongside my two guardian angels, Pauline and Peggy, my liaisons who would be assisting me on the entire trip. I was going back to Poland as part of the March of the Living, an annual silent commemorative march from Auschwitz to Birkenau, which helps educate the younger generation about what so many of us experienced all those years ago.

I didn't show it, but I was scared and anxious. I was about to face the places that signify so much loss. Krakow ghetto is where I witnessed the murder of my whole family, and I will never forget the horrors I experienced at the Plaszow camp, Auschwitz, Birkenau and so many others. How was I going to tell these wonderful kids about the atrocities of these places? I had decided that they needed to know — it had to be done.

Finally, we boarded the plane heading to Toronto, where we would join all the wonderful kids, chaperones and staff who would be going on the march from Canada. During the flight, I felt a sense of calmness and finally felt ready to open up and share this part of my life that I never thought I would share. When we landed in Toronto, we were greeted with an overwhelming amount of love, respect and warmth. There are no words to describe the feeling of meeting this amazing group. I was treated as if I were a celebrity.

We were humbled as we boarded our flight to Krakow, Poland, when we realized that all the survivors were seated in first class. This was a real treat for the eight-hour flight.

As we descended into the Krakow airport, it felt surreal to be looking out the window at my place of birth. We arrived at 12:45 p.m., which meant we had been already travelling for more than twenty-four hours without any sleep. How could I have slept knowing what I was about to embark on? I felt so excited to be back in my hometown after seventy-five years. I did not feel tired; in fact, I felt awake and ready to meet the challenge ahead.

As we entered the Krakow airport, I was met by the documentary crew headed by Naomi Wise. I was separated from the kids, which I felt uneasy about, since my main goal was to share everything with these participants. Regardless, I followed the crew as we got into separate taxis and headed to Zamenhofa Street, where I was born. I built many happy memories on this street with my family and spent my childhood there until I turned thirteen years old, when we were forced to move by the Germans.

I entered the cab and felt as though I was having an out-of-body experience. Here I was, after seventy-five years, directing our driver on the fastest way to get to our destination, and doing so in perfect Polish. I told the driver about my return to Krakow, and he couldn't believe that it was my first time back after so long. In a bizarre way, I felt as though I had never left. I repeatedly said to myself, "I am back."

After a short drive, we arrived at my old street, and I felt speechless, like my breath had been taken away. I felt happy and couldn't help but smile. Here I was, standing in front of the apartment where I was born and grew up. My mind suddenly flooded with so many memories and flashbacks. After all, I spent thirteen years in this home surrounded by my family. It felt hard to believe that all these years had gone by since then — it was almost like the years disappeared, and I felt myself returning to 1939.

We then went to Szpitalna Street, which was a few blocks away from the old part of Krakow. We went with the goal of visiting the synagogue where my older brother had had his bar mitzvah. This exact synagogue was where I was supposed to have had mine as well. I showed the crew a nightclub next door called Cyganeria, which had been frequented by the Germans. I distinctly remember when the boys from the ghetto threw a bomb into the nightclub and succeeded in killing quite a few Germans. I made sure to point out the plaque in front of the nightclub commemorating this Jewish partisan moment. I felt myself going back and forth between the past and the present. After visiting my childhood street and the nightclub, I felt that it was time to reunite with the young people from the March of the Living.

We went to join the group, who were waiting for me in front of the old synagogue in Kazimierz. I was asked to speak to them about my experience growing up, so I did. It was wonderful to talk to them about it. I felt an overwhelming amount of love for them, and I received that same amount of love in return.

The next stop on the itinerary was Plaszow (in the suburbs of Krakow), the site of the forced labour and concentration camp built on a former Jewish cemetery, where the headstones were used to build the roads. It was shocking to see that the camp now looked like a beautiful picnic ground. As I walked up the hill, I felt a rush of exhaustion, as we had been travelling for what felt like forever. Halfway up the hill, I met a group of kids from Morocco. The leader of the group requested that I share my story. They told me, "We have never met a survivor." I looked around and responded, "Do I look different?" The supervisor of the Moroccan delegation laughed and seemed to appreciate my humour. I decided to stay with the Moroccan group and share my story, as the survivor liaisons Peggy and Pauline stayed by my side.

We did all of this on the first day, which wasn't over yet. At around 6:00 p.m., we arrived back at the old synagogue in Kazimierz, where I participated in lighting six candles in memory of the six million Jews who were murdered in the Holocaust.

Finally, after forty-eight hours, our bus took us to the hotel so we could check in. I put my head on the pillow and fell asleep.

On our second day in Poland we participated in the March of the Living from Auschwitz to Birkenau, with young people and students from all around the world. I was scared but tried not to show my emotions. The bus trip from Krakow to Auschwitz was only about an hour and a half, and I started to remember the same trip on February 20, 1944, going from the Plaszow camp to Auschwitz, a trip that took two days and nights in a sealed cattle car without any food or water or place to relieve ourselves. Arriving in Auschwitz, or rather Birkenau, we were met by guards who beat us with whips, and barking dogs, forcing us to run to Auschwitz.

This was going to be a different experience. We marched with dignitaries (the Polish president, Israeli president and many others) in an orderly fashion, from Auschwitz to Birkenau. In Auschwitz, I showed the young people and everybody else blocks 18 and 19, where I survived for one year. Then I told them about my first day there, standing naked in the snow for hours. Somehow I stayed calm as I talked about these experiences, as though I was talking about somebody else. But when we arrived in Birkenau and I saw the railway cars, all my memories came rushing back. I felt again the fear of being beaten by the guards, of dogs jumping on me. I heard the screaming and yelling, "Schnell! Schnell! Raus, verfluchte Juden!" (Fast! Fast! Out, cursed Jews!). The feeling lasted with me for a while.

The next day, day three, we were off to Warsaw.

Going through the countryside, I was impressed with the progress since I had left. At that time, the houses in the villages had roofs made of straw, a cow or two in the front and sometimes a horse. Now there were modern houses with cars in front.

I opened my mouth in awe as we approached Warsaw, seeing the most modern city I have ever seen. In the afternoon, the survivors took a walk in the old city, which had been completely rebuilt after the war.

⁓

The fourth day of the trip was Saturday. Because it was the Sabbath, the day of rest, we were finally able to rest and relax with the wonderful kids, chaperones, staff, Peggy and Pauline.

⁓

Seventy-nine years ago, in 1939, I began preparing for my bar mitzvah. The war then broke out, and Germany invaded Poland. Here I was at ninety-two years of age back in Poland for the first time since World War II. Not only was I here to go on the March of the Living, but I was also finally going to celebrate my bar mitzvah in the country I had been forced to leave so long ago.

As Rabbi Pinny Gniwisch (who encouraged me to have my bar mitzvah) said, "This is your revenge. You owe it to yourself to reclaim what was taken from you."

And this was my big day!

I was going to have my bar mitzvah in the oldest, most well-preserved synagogue in northeastern Poland, in the small town of Tykocin, which now had about two thousand inhabitants. The historic synagogue in Tykocin was built in 1642. The town had a Jewish population of about two thousand before the war, but this entire population was murdered, shot by the Germans on August 25, 1941, in the nearby forest.

When we arrived in the town, there was not even one soul on the street. In the synagogue itself, I was seated on the *bimah*, surrounded by all the wonderful young people from the March of the Living, as well as the chaperones, staff, Rabbi Pinny Gniwisch and my dearest Pauline and Peggy.

It is almost impossible to tell how I felt. Ecstatic, happy, like I had never felt before in my life. Crying inside, smiling on the outside. Experiencing so much love. I was only very sorry that my dearest daughter, Debbie, and my grandson, Daniel, could not be with me.

Soon it was over, and I had reached my goal.

I have my revenge and now it is time for these wonderful kids to keep the memories alive.

It is exactly seventy-nine years since German troops invaded Poland and World War II began. I still remember that day like it was yesterday. For me it was the day the Holocaust started, and I continue to have nightmares about it. We should always remember what people are capable of doing to one another and try to prevent it from happening again.

I still don't comprehend how such a cultured and highly educated nation like Germany could commit to and execute such a diabolic plan to murder a whole nation — children, women, everybody — just because they were Jewish. It is an atrocity unparalleled in the history of humankind.

I will finish my memoir with these words:

May we always pay homage to the dead, so that they remain a warning to the living.

Weisberg & Jablon Glossary

Aktion (German; pl. *Aktionen*) The brutal roundup of Jews for forced labour, forcible resettlement into ghettos, mass murder by shooting or deportation to death camps.

aliyah (Hebrew; pl. *aliyot*, literally, ascent) A term used by Jews and modern Israelis to refer to Jewish immigration to Israel; the term is also used to refer to "going up" to the altar in a synagogue to read from the Torah.

Appell (also *Zählappell*) (German) Roll call.

Appellplatz (German; the place for roll call) The area in Nazi camps where inmates had to assemble to be counted. Roll calls were part of a series of daily humiliations for prisoners, who were often made to stand completely still for hours, regardless of the weather conditions.

Auschwitz (German; in Polish, Oświęcim) A town in southern Poland approximately 40 kilometres from Krakow, it is also the name of the largest complex of Nazi concentration camps that were built nearby. The Auschwitz complex contained three main camps: Auschwitz I, a slave labour camp built in May 1940; Auschwitz II-Birkenau, a death camp built in early 1942; and Auschwitz-Monowitz, a slave labour camp built in October 1942. In 1941, Auschwitz I was a testing site for usage of the lethal gas

Zyklon B as a method of mass killing, which then went into wide usage. Between 1942 and 1944, transports arrived at Auschwitz-Birkenau from almost every country in Europe — hundreds of thousands from both Poland and Hungary, and thousands from France, the Netherlands, Greece, Slovakia, Bohemia and Moravia, Yugoslavia, Belgium, Italy and Norway. As well, more than 30,000 people were deported there from other concentration camps. It is estimated that 1.1 million people were murdered in Auschwitz; approximately 950,000 were Jewish; 74,000 Polish; 21,000 Roma; 15,000 Soviet prisoners of war; and 10,000–15,000 other nationalities. The Auschwitz complex was liberated by the Soviet army in January 1945.

bar mitzvah (Hebrew; literally, son of the commandment) The time when, in Jewish tradition, children become religiously and morally responsible for their actions and are considered adults for the purpose of synagogue and other rituals. Traditionally this occurs at age thirteen for boys. A bar mitzvah is also the synagogue ceremony and family celebration that mark the attainment of this status, during which the boy is called upon to read a portion of the Torah and recite the prescribed prayers in a public prayer service.

Bełżec A death camp that was established in 1942 in the Lublin district, Poland. Bełżec was the first of three death camps built specifically for the implementation of Operation Reinhard, the German code word for the Nazi plan for the mass murder of Jews in occupied Poland. Between March and December 1942, approximately 600,000 Jews were murdered in Bełżec.

Bergen-Belsen A camp initially established by the Nazis in 1940 for prisoners of war near Celle, Germany. After 1943, it held so-called exchange Jews in the "residence camp" and "star camp" whom Germany hoped to use in peace negotiations with the Allies, as well as to trade for German nationals. By December 1944, Bergen-Belsen was designated a concentration camp and comprised various subcamps for different categories of prisoners. Toward the end of the war, thousands of prisoners from camps close to the front lines, such as Auschwitz, Mittelbau-Dora and Buchenwald were taken to Bergen-Belsen, as were forced labourers from Hungary. With the influx of inmates, camp conditions deteriorated rapidly and some 35,000 people died between January and April 1945. British forces liberated the camp on April 15, 1945. After the war, Bergen-Belsen became a Displaced Persons camp, from 1945 to 1950.

Betar A Zionist youth movement founded by Revisionist Zionist leader Ze'ev Jabotinsky in 1923 that encouraged the development of a new generation of Zionist activists based on the ideals of courage, self-respect, military training, defence of Jewish life and property, and settlement in Israel to establish a Jewish state in British Mandate Palestine. In 1934, Betar membership in Poland numbered more than 40,000. During the 1930s and 1940s, as antisemitism increased and the Nazis launched their murderous campaign against the Jews of Europe, Betar rescued thousands of Jews by organizing illegal immigration to British Mandate Palestine. The Betar movement today, closely aligned with Israel's right-wing Likud party, remains involved in supporting Jewish and Zionist activism around the world.

Blue Police The Polish police during World War II in the General Government. The pre-war Polish police force was mobilized to serve the occupying German government. The police force existed from October 30, 1939, to August 27, 1944. *See also* General Government.

bimah (Hebrew) The raised platform in a synagogue from which the Torah is read.

Bindermichl DP camp A Displaced Persons camp located in Linz, Austria, that housed approximately 2,500 people from October 1945 to March 1949. The Bindermichl camp was a social and cultural community for displaced Jews of post-war Europe. There were educational facilities and religious organizations, and newspapers produced by the residents were distributed to other DP camps in Austria. The Jewish Historical Commission, which documented war crimes, was established there; it later became Simon Wiesenthal's Jewish Historical Documentation Centre.

British Mandate Palestine The area of the Middle East under British rule from 1923 to 1948, as established by the League of Nations after World War I. During that time, the United Kingdom severely restricted Jewish immigration. The Mandate area encompassed present-day Israel, Jordan, the West Bank and the Gaza Strip.

Canadian Jewish Congress (CJC) An advocacy organization and lobbying group for the Canadian Jewish community from 1919 to 2011. In 1947, the CJC convinced the Canadian government to re-issue Privy Council Order 1647 — originally adopted in 1942 to admit 500 Jewish refugee children from Vichy France, although they never made it out — that allowed for 1,000 Jewish children under the age of eighteen to be admitted to Canada. The CJC was restructured in 2007 and its functions subsumed under the Centre for Israel and Jewish Affairs (CIJA) in 2011. *See also* War Orphans Project; United Nations Relief and Rehabilitation Administration (UNRRA).

cantor (in Hebrew, *chazzan*) A person who leads a Jewish congregation in prayer. Because music plays such a large role in Jewish religious services, the cantor is usually professionally trained in music.

cattle cars Freight cars used to deport Jews by rail to concentration camps and death camps. The European railways played a key logistical role in how the Nazis were able to transport millions of Jews from around Europe to killing centres in occupied Poland under the guise of "relocation." The train cars were usually ten metres long and often crammed with more than a hundred people in abhorrent conditions with no water, food or sanitation. Many Jews, already weak from poor living conditions in the ghettos, died in the train cars from suffocation or illness before ever arriving at the camps.

chai (Hebrew; literally, living) Word comprised of the Hebrew letters *chet* and *yod*, the eighth and tenth letters of the alphabet, thus corresponding to the numerical value of 18 (which therefore represents the concept of life in Jewish tradition). The two Hebrew letters form a symbol that is often worn as a jewellery pendant and considered a good luck charm. Derivatives of *chai*, such as Chaim (male) or Chaya (female), are common Jewish first names.

Chumash (Hebrew; from *chamesh*, five) The Pentateuch. The term is used to refer to the Five Books of Moses when they are in book form, as distinct from the Sefer Torah. *See also* Sefer Torah; Torah.

Cyrankiewicz, Józef (1911–1989) Polish Socialist and Communist politician and prime minister of the People's Republic of Poland from 1947 to 1952 and again from 1954 to 1970. Born in Tarnów in what was then the Austro-Hungarian Empire (now southeastern Poland), Cyrankiewicz was involved in the Polish resistance organization Armia Krajowa during World War II. After having been captured and then escaping from the Germans early in the war, he was then captured a second time in 1941 and imprisoned in Auschwitz until the end of the war.

death march A term that refers to the forced travel of prisoners who were evacuated from various Nazi camps near the end of the war. Prisoners often had to walk thousands of kilometres under difficult conditions and many died of starvation, exhaustion, exposure, or at the hands of SS guards if they collapsed or could not keep up with others on the march.

displaced persons (DPs) People who find themselves homeless and stateless at the end of a war. Following World War II, millions of people, especially European Jews, found that they had no homes to return to or that it was unsafe to do so. To resolve the staggering refugee crisis that resulted, Allied authorities and the United Nations Relief and Rehabilitation Administration (UNRRA) established Displaced Persons (DP) camps to provide temporary shelter and assistance to refugees, and help them transition toward resettlement. *See also* DP camps.

DP camps Facilities set up by the Allied authorities and the United Nations Relief and Rehabilitation Administration (UNRRA) in October 1945 to resolve the refugee crisis that arose at the end of World War II. The camps provided temporary shelter and assistance to the millions of people — not only Jews — who had been displaced from their home countries as a result of the war and helped them prepare for resettlement. *See also* United Nations Relief and Rehabilitation Administration (UNRRA).

Falkenberg Founded in late April or early May 1944, a subcamp of Gross-Rosen set up in the village of Ludwigsdorf and named after the larger nearby village of Falkenberg in Germany. Life in the camp was marked by terrible living conditions and hard labour, resulting not only in the physical but also the mental degradation of the prisoners, which led to many suicides in the camp. The prisoner labour was primarily used by the Organisation Todt. The camp was disbanded in February 1945, with the existing prisoners transferred to other camps. *See also* Gross-Rosen; Organisation Todt.

Gemara (Aramaic; literally, study) One of two parts of the Talmud, the other being the Mishnah, the Gemara is based on the discussions of generations of sages in Babylonia and Israel. It serves to clarify the Mishnah and provide examples of how to apply legal opinions.

General Government (also *Generalgouvernement*) The territory in central Poland that was conquered by the Germans in September 1939 but not annexed to the Third Reich. Made up of the districts of Warsaw, Krakow, Radom and Lublin, it was deemed a special administrative area and was used as the place for the Nazis to carry out their racial plans of murdering Jews. From 1939 onward, Jews from all over German-occupied territories were transferred to this region, as were Poles who had been expelled from their homes in the annexed Polish territories further west.

ghetto A confined residential area for Jews. The term originated in Venice, Italy, in 1516 with a law requiring all Jews to live on a segregated, gated island known as Ghetto Nuovo. Throughout the Middle Ages in Europe, Jews were often forcibly confined to gated Jewish neighbourhoods. During the Holocaust, the Nazis forced Jews to live in crowded and unsanitary conditions in run-down districts of cities and towns. Most ghettos in Poland were enclosed by brick walls or wooden fences with barbed wire.

Göth, Amon (1908–1946) Austrian Nazi captain and commandant of the Plaszow forced labour and concentration camp. Göth was infamous for his volatile nature and brutality against Jews. He murdered and tortured thousands of Jews and was hanged for his crimes in 1946 under a ruling by the Supreme National Tribunal of Poland.

Gross-Rosen A village in western Poland, now named Rogoźnica, where a labour camp was established in 1940. Prisoners were forced to construct camp barracks and work in a nearby quarry. As the camp was expanded to include armaments production, Gross-Rosen became classified as a concentration camp and was the centre of a complex of at least ninety-seven subcamps. As of January 1945, 76,728 prisoners were held there, of whom about one-third were women, mostly Jews. Liquidation of the subcamps began in January 1945 and Gross-Rosen was evacuated in early February 1945, with 40,000 prisoners, including 20,000 Jews, being forced on death marches. The camp was liberated by the Soviet Red Army on February 13, 1945. It is estimated that 120,000 prisoners passed through the Gross-Rosen camp complex; 40,000 died either in Gross-Rosen or during its liquidation.

Gunskirchen A subcamp of the Mauthausen-Gusen complex that was built in December 1944 and held more than 16,000 Hungarians, hundreds of political prisoners, and, in April 1945, thousands of Jews who had been transferred from the Mauthausen camp. The camp was located in Upper Austria north of the town of Gunskirchen and outside the village of Edt bei Lambach. Due to the camp's immense overcrowding and unsanitary conditions, between 200 and 300 inmates died there each day from typhoid fever and dysentery. Gunskirchen was liberated by American troops on May 4, 1945.

Gusen One of the fifty subcamps in the Mauthausen-Gusen complex, Gusen was started in December 1939 and had about 200 prisoner workers by January 1940. Gusen quickly became a large facility. Resulting from the arrival of prisoners from liquidated camps in the east, by May 1945 there were 20,487 prisoners in the camp, vastly exceeding its original capacity of 4,000 to 5,000 prisoners. The overcrowded camp lacked sanitary drinking water and other basic facilities and was known as "the hell of hells"; the average lifespan of a Gusen inmate was about four months. In March 1944 — after Allied bombs had bombed the Messerschmitt aircraft factory in southern Germany — Gusen II was founded to house an underground war production plant. By September 1944, Gusen II held 10,000 prisoners, most of whom worked in the underground factory. Inmates were used to excavate tunnels and perform other laborious tasks to construct the plant, after which they then began building fuselages for the mass production of fighter jets. A smaller subcamp that held about 260 prisoners, Gusen III, was also added in December 1944.

Hasidic Judaism (from the Hebrew word *hasid*; literally, piety) An Orthodox Jewish spiritual movement founded by Rabbi Israel ben Eliezer (1698–1760), better known as the Baal Shem Tov, in eighteenth-century Poland. The Hasidic movement, characterized by philosophies of mysticism and focusing on joyful prayer, resulted in a new kind of leader who attracted disciples as opposed to the traditional rabbis who focused on the intellectual study of Jewish law.

Hebrew Immigrant Aid Society (HIAS) An organization founded in New York in 1881 that continues to provide aid, counsel, support and general assistance to Jewish immigrants all over the world. Since the early 1970s, HIAS has been especially active in providing assistance to Jews emigrating from the USSR.

High Holidays (also High Holy Days) The autumn holidays that mark the beginning of the Jewish year and that include Rosh Hashanah (New Year) and Yom Kippur (Day of Atonement). *See also* Rosh Hashanah.

Hujowa Górka (Polish; Hujar's Hill) A site of mass murder and burials in the Plaszow concentration camp named after a vicious SS officer, Albert Hujar. In April 1944, the Germans attempted to hide the evidence of these murders by exhuming and incinerating the bodies buried here.

Judenrat (German; pl. *Judenräte*) Jewish Council. A group of Jewish leaders appointed by the Germans to administer and provide services to the local Jewish population under occupation and carry out Nazi orders. The *Judenräte*, which appeared to be self-governing entities but were actually under complete Nazi control, faced difficult and complex moral decisions under brutal conditions and remain a contentious subject. The chairmen had to decide whether to comply or refuse to comply with Nazi demands. Some were killed by the Nazis for refusing, while others committed suicide. Jewish officials who advocated compliance thought that cooperation might save at least some of the population. Some who denounced resistance efforts did so because they believed that armed resistance would bring death to the entire community.

Jüdischer Ordnungsdienst (German; literally, Jewish Order Service) The Jewish ghetto police force established by the Jewish Councils on the orders of the Germans. The force was armed with clubs and was created to carry out various tasks in the ghettos, such as traffic control and guarding the ghetto gates. Eventually, some policemen also participated in rounding up Jews for forced labour and transportation to the death camps. There has been much debate and controversy surrounding the role of both the Jewish Councils and the Jewish police. Even though the Jewish police exercised considerable power within the ghetto, to the Germans these policemen were still Jews and subject to the same fate as other Jews.

Kanada The warehouses in Auschwitz that stored the belongings and clothing confiscated from newly arrived prisoners. The name, adopted by the prisoners working there, came from the widely held belief that Canada was a land of wealth, thus its association with the enormous amount of goods seized by the camp authorities.

kapo (German) A concentration camp prisoner appointed by the SS to oversee other prisoners as slave labourers.

Kommando (German; literally, unit or command) Forced work details that were set up by the Nazi labour and concentration camp administrators during World War II. Sam Weisberg uses the term to refer to those who had work placements outside the camp, though the term is also used for workers inside labour and concentration camps.

Konzentrationslager (German; concentration camp). Often abbreviated as KZ.

Krakow ghetto An area established in March 1941 in the Podgórze district of Krakow where more than 15,000 Jews were forced to live in a confined space that had previously housed only 3,000 people. The Nazis dissolved the ghetto on March 13, 1943, and deported 6,000 Jews to the forced labour camp at Płaszów. *See also* Plaszow.

Ma Nishtana (Hebrew; literally, what is different?) The first words of the Four Questions asked during the Passover seder and often performed as a song, usually by the youngest child at the table. As much of the seder is designed to fulfill the biblical obligation to tell the Exodus story to children, the ritual of asking the Four Questions is one of the most important at the seder. The questions revolve around the theme of how this night of commemoration of the Exodus is different from other nights — e.g., Why do we eat unleavened bread? Why do we eat bitter herbs? The readings that follow answer the questions and in doing so tell the Exodus story. *See also* Passover; seder.

Mauthausen A notoriously brutal Nazi concentration camp located about 20 kilometres east of the Austrian city of Linz. First established in 1938 shortly after the annexation of Austria to imprison "asocial" political opponents of the Third Reich, the camp grew to encompass fifty nearby subcamps and became the largest forced labour complex in the German-occupied territories. By the end of the war, close to 200,000 prisoners had passed through the Mauthausen forced labour camp system and almost 120,000 of them died there — including 38,120 Jews — from starvation, disease and hard labour. Mauthausen was classified as a Category 3 camp, which indicated the harshest conditions, and inmates were often worked to death in the brutal Weiner-Graben stone quarry. The US army liberated the camp on May 5, 1945.

Melk An Austrian town about 100 kilometres east of the city of Linz that was also the site of one of the subcamps of the Mauthausen concentration camp complex. The Melk subcamp existed from April 1944 until April 1945 and functioned as a forced labour camp that used prisoners to build quartz tunnels in the surrounding mountains. More than 10,000 people died in Melk, which also had a gas chamber and a crematorium.

Mengele, Josef (1911–1979) The most notorious of about thirty SS garrison physicians in Auschwitz. Mengele was stationed at the camp from May 1943 to January 1945; from May 1943 to August 1944, he was the medical officer of the Birkenau "Gypsy Camp"; from August 1944 until Auschwitz was evacuated in January 1945, he was Chief Medical Officer of the main infirmary camp in Birkenau. One of the camp doctors responsible for deciding which prisoners were fit for slave labour and which were to be immediately sent to the gas chambers, Mengele was also known for conducting sadistic experiments on Jewish and Roma prisoners, especially twins.

mikvah (Hebrew; literally, a pool or gathering of water) A ritual purification bath taken by Jews on occasions that denote change, such as before the Sabbath (signifying the shift from a regular weekday to a holy day of rest), as well as those that denote a change in personal status, such as before a person's wedding or, for a married woman, after menstruation. The word mikvah refers to both the pool of water and the building that houses the ritual bath.

Muselmann (plural, Muselmänner; German; Muslim) A slang term used by camp prisoners to describe prisoners who were near death and seemed to have lost the will to live. Some scholars attribute the use of the word Muslim to the fact that the prostrate and dying prisoners were reminiscent of devout Muslims at prayer.

NKVD (Russian) The acronym of the Narodnyi Komissariat Vnutrennikh Del, meaning People's Commissariat for Internal Affairs. The NKVD functioned as the Soviet Union's security agency, secret police and intelligence agency from 1934 to 1954. The NKVD's Main Directorate for State Security (GUGB) was the forerunner of the Committee for State Security, better known as the KGB (acronym for Komitet Gosudarstvennoy Bezopasnosti) established in 1954. The organization's stated dual purpose was to defend the USSR from external dangers from foreign powers and to protect the Communist Party from perceived dangers within. Under Stalin, the pursuit of imagined conspiracies against the state became a central focus, and the NKVD played a critical role in suppressing political dissent.

Oberscharführer (German; senior squad leader; pl. *Oberscharfürerin*) A Nazi SS party rank between 1932 and 1945. *See also* SS.

Oberwachtmeister (German; senior sergeant) A non-commissioned officer (NCO) rank in the German army and air force equivalent to sergeant. After 1945, the term *Oberfeldwebel* was used for this rank.

Occupation of Poland Germany invaded Poland on September 1, 1939, and swiftly took control of Warsaw with aerial bombardments, and of Krakow, Katowice and Tunel with the use of firebombs. On September 17, the Soviet Union occupied Eastern Poland. By September 27, Polish government leaders and thousands of Polish troops escaped to neutral Romania; by October 6, Poland had been completely occupied and divided between Germany and the Soviet Union. *See also* Treaty of Non-Aggression between Germany and the USSR.

Organisation Todt A construction and civil engineering group named for its founder, Fritz Todt, that undertook major civilian and military projects under the Nazis. It began as a quasi-governmental agency but in 1942 it was absorbed by the German government, becoming part of the Ministry of Armaments and War Production under Albert Speer. The Organisation Todt made extensive use of forced and slave labour during the war.

Organization for Rehabilitation through Training (ORT) A vocational school system founded for Jews by Jews in Russia in 1880. The name ORT derives from the acronym of the Russian organization Obshestvo Remeslenogo Zemledelcheskogo Truda, Society for Trades and Agricultural Labour.

organize A Nazi camp term that meant illegally acquiring everyday objects of benefit to inmates, such as food, clothing and medicines.

Orthodox Judaism The set of beliefs and practices of Jews for whom the observance of Jewish law is closely connected to faith; it is characterized by strict religious observance of Jewish dietary laws, restrictions on work on the Sabbath and holidays, and a code of modesty in dress.

Passover (in Hebrew, Pesach) One of the major festivals of the Jewish calendar, Passover takes place over eight days in the spring. One of the main observances of the holiday is to recount the story of Exodus, the Jews' flight from slavery in Egypt, at a ritual meal called a seder. The name itself refers to the fact that God "passed over" the houses of the Jews when he set about slaying the firstborn sons of Egypt as the last of the ten plagues aimed at convincing Pharaoh to free the Jews. *See also* Ma Nishtana; seder.

Plaszow A labour camp constructed on two Jewish cemeteries in a suburb of Krakow in 1942 and enlarged to become a concentration camp in January 1944. Plaszow was also used as a transit camp

— more than 150,000 people passed through the camp, many en route to Auschwitz. About 80,000 were murdered in the camp itself, either by execution or through hard labour. By mid-1944, Plaszow held more than 20,000 prisoners; inmates were used for slave labour in the quarry or railway construction and were subject to the volatile whims of camp commandant Amon Göth, who was personally responsible for more than 8,000 deaths. *See also* Göth, Amon.

Poale Zion (Hebrew, also Poalei Zion; Workers of Zion) A Marxist-Jewish Zionist movement founded in the Russian Empire in the early twentieth century.

Ravitch, Melech (pseudonym of Zekharye Khone Bergner; 1893–1976) A modernist Yiddish poet who was born in Radymno, eastern Galicia. Ravitch became involved with a movement to preserve Yiddish as the language of the Jewish people at the age of fifteen. He settled in Montreal in 1941, where he became involved in the Yiddish intellectual life of the city, helping to foster a postwar Yiddish culture in Montreal.

Red Army (in Russian, *Krasnaya Armiya*) A term used from 1918 to 1946 for the Soviet Union's armed forces, which were founded when the Bolshevik Party came to power after the Russian Revolution. The original name was the Workers' and Peasants' Red Army, the colour red representing blood spilled while struggling against oppression.

Rosh Hashanah (Hebrew) New Year. The autumn holiday that marks the beginning of the Jewish year and ushers in the High Holy Days. It is observed by a synagogue service that ends with blowing the *shofar* (ram's horn), which marks the beginning of the holiday. The service is usually followed by a family dinner where sweet foods, such as apples and honey, are eaten to symbolize and celebrate a sweet new year.

Schindler, Oskar (1908–1974) The German businessman who saved the lives of more than 1,000 Jews, who are often referred to as *Schindlerjuden* (Schindler's Jews). Schindler, a member of the Nazi Party, took over an enamel factory situated close to the Plaszow labour camp in 1940 and began employing Jewish workers there, sheltering them from the harsh conditions at the camp. Though Schindler profited from the cheap labour, he was increasingly motivated to preserve the lives of his workers and went to extreme lengths to save them from death, often advocating for them and bribing camp commandant Amon Göth and other Nazi officials who came to inspect the factory. When his enamel factory, Deutsche Emailwaren Fabrik, was forced to close in 1944 as the Soviet troops advanced, he heroically rescued more than 1,000 Jews from deportation to Auschwitz by declaring them to be "essential to the war effort" and transporting them to his new munitions factory in Brünnlitz, Sudetenland. Oskar Schindler was awarded the title of Righteous Among the Nations by Yad Vashem in 1993 and was the subject of Steven Spielberg's 1993 film *Schindler's List*, based on the novel *Schindler's Ark* by Thomas Keneally.

seder (Hebrew; literally, order) A ritual family meal celebrated at the beginning of the festival of Passover. *See also* Ma Nisthanah; Passover.

Sefer Torah (Hebrew) A handwritten copy of the Torah in the form of a scroll traditionally stored in a synagogue to be used during services. A printed and bound copy is known as a Chumash. *See also* Chumash; Torah.

shmatte (Yiddish; literally, rag) A term that refers to the garment industry.

Sonderkommando (German; special unit) Concentration camp prisoners ordered to remove corpses from the gas chambers, load them into the crematoria and dispose of the remains. On October 7, 1944, *Sonderkommando* workers coordinated an attempt to destroy the crematoria facilities at Auschwitz-Birkenau.

SS (abbreviation of Schutzstaffel; Defence Corps) The SS was established in 1925 as Adolf Hitler's elite corps of personal bodyguards. Under the direction of Heinrich Himmler, its membership grew from 280 in 1929 to 50,000 when the Nazis came to power in 1933, and to nearly a quarter of a million on the eve of World War II. The SS was comprised of the Allgemeine-SS (General SS) and the Waffen-SS (Armed, or Combat SS). The General SS dealt with policing and the enforcement of Nazi racial policies in Germany and the Nazi-occupied countries. The SS ran the concentration and death camps, with all their associated economic enterprises, and also fielded its own Waffen-SS military divisions, including some recruited from the occupied countries.

Star of David (in Hebrew, Magen David) The six-pointed star that is the ancient and most recognizable symbol of Judaism. During World War II, Jews in Nazi-occupied areas were frequently forced to wear a badge or armband with the Star of David on it as an identifying mark of their lesser status and to single them out as targets for persecution.

tefillin (Hebrew) Phylacteries. A pair of black leather boxes containing scrolls of parchment inscribed with Bible verses and worn by Jews on the arm and forehead at prescribed times of prayer as a symbol of the covenantal relationship with God.

Torah (Hebrew) The Five Books of Moses (the first five books of the Bible), also called the Pentateuch. The Torah is the core of Jewish scripture, traditionally believed to have been given to Moses on Mount Sinai. In Christianity it is referred to as the "Old Testament." *See also* Chumash; Sefer Torah.

Treaty of Non-Aggression between Germany and the USSR The treaty that was signed on August 24, 1939, and was colloquially known as the Molotov-Ribbentrop pact, after signatories Soviet foreign minister Vyacheslav Molotov and German foreign minister Joachim von Ribbentrop. The main provisions of the pact stipulated that the two countries would not go to war with each other and that they would both remain neutral if either one was attacked by a third party. One of the key components of the treaty was the division of various independent countries — including Poland — into Nazi and Soviet spheres of influence and areas of occupation. The Nazis breached the pact by launching a major offensive against the Soviet Union on June 22, 1941.

United Nations Relief and Rehabilitation Administration (UNRRA) An international relief agency created at a 44-nation conference in Washington, DC, on November 9, 1943, to provide economic assistance and basic necessities to war refugees. It was especially active in repatriating and assisting refugees in the formerly Nazi-occupied European nations immediately after World War II.

War Orphans Project Under the auspices of the Canadian Jewish Congress (CJC), which would provide for the refugees' care, the War Orphans Project was established in April 1947, and the CJC began searching for Jewish war orphans with the help of the United Nations Relief and Rehabilitation Administration (UNRRA). Between 1947 and 1949, 1,123 young Jewish refugees came to Canada. *See also* Canadian Jewish Congress (CJC); United Nations Relief and Rehabilitation Administration (UNRRA).

Zwangsarbeitslager (German) Forced labour camp.

Photographs

Sam Weisberg

1 Sam's mother, Esther Etel, before the war. Krakow, Poland, date unknown.
2 Sam (then called Avraham, right) with his brother, Yehezkel Yosef. Chorzów, Poland, circa 1935.
3 Sam and his immediate family. From left to right: Sam's mother, Esther Etel; his brother, Yehezkel Yosef; Sam; and his father, Eli Meyer. Chorzów, Poland, circa 1935.

Sam, age seventeen, after the war in the Bergen-Belsen Displaced Persons camp. Germany, 1945.

1 Sam's fiancée, Rosa (then Bronka), in the Bergen-Belsen DP camp. Germany, circa 1945.
2 Sam in the DP camp, circa 1945.
3 Sam (far left, facing camera) standing beside the car provided to him by the British army for his work as an interpreter. Bergen-Belsen, Germany, circa 1946.

Sam and Rosa enjoying a bike ride through the DP camp. Bergen-Belsen, Germany, circa 1947.

1 Sam and Rosa (third and fourth from the left) at their pre-wedding party. Bergen-Belsen, Germany, 1946.
2 The double wedding in the DP camp. From left to right: Leo, Luba, Rosa and Sam. Bergen-Belsen, Germany, August 21, 1946.

1 Rosa and her brother, Rachmiel (Ralph) Horowitz. Bergen-Belsen, Germany, circa 1946.
2 Sam's only surviving family, the Spieglers, on their way to Israel. From left to right: Sam's cousin Avraham; his aunt Bela; his wife, Rosa; and his cousin Chaim. Bergen-Belsen, Germany, circa 1948.
3 Sam with his family in Bergen-Belsen, Germany. In back, left to right: Avraham, Rachmiel and Chaim. In front, left to right: Rosa, Bela and Sam. Circa 1948.

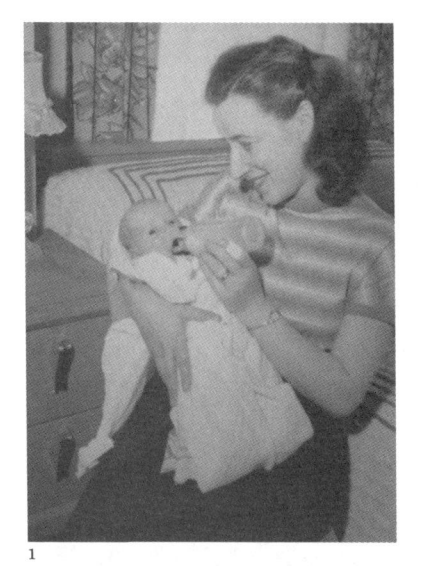

1　Rosa with her and Sam's newborn daughter, Sharon. Canton, Ohio, 1952.
2　Rosa's aunt Monia with one-year-old Sharon, 1953.
3　Sam and Rosa's children, Sharon and Max. Toronto, circa 1962.

The Weisberg family at a celebration. Toronto, circa 1967.

Sam at the Radomer memorial monument at Dawes Road Cemetery, established by B'nai Radom. Toronto, circa 1960s.

Sam's son, Max, and daughter-in-law, Lynda, on their wedding day. Toronto, June 12, 1983.

1 Sam (centre) and his family with then Minister of Citizenship Cam Jackson (far right) at the ceremony where he was honoured by the government of Ontario as a Holocaust survivor committed to Holocaust remembrance. Toronto, 2001.
2 Sam and family at the ceremony where he was honoured by the government of Ontario. Toronto, 2001.

1 Sam's daughter, Sharon Jesin, and her husband, Aaron. Israel, spring 2018.
2 Sam's grandson Shlomo Jesin. Israel, spring 2018.
3 Sam's grandson Yehezkel Jesin and his wife, Rebecca, with their children, Hailey, Max and Jack. USA, spring 2018.
4 Sam's grandson Raphael Jesin and his wife, Rachel, with their newborn son, Ilan, Sam's eighteenth great-grandchild. USA, 2018.

1 Sam's granddaughter Ahuva Balofsky and her husband, Meir (far right), with their children, Shoshana, Ariel and Moshe. Israel, spring 2018.
2 Sam's granddaughter Maytal Allman and her husband, Safi, with their children, Ayelet, Maya, Talia and Noa. Israel, spring 2018.

Sam's granddaughter Aliza Abrahamovitz and her husband, David, with their children. In the back, from left to right: Chani, Elisheva and Nava; in front, from left to right: Akiva, Adina, Moshe-Chaim and Noam. Israel, spring 2018.

1 Sam Weisberg and his wife, Rosa. Muskoka, Ontario, 2008.
2 Sam Weisberg. Toronto, 2018.

Johnny Jablon

Johnny's mother, Dora (née Ormian) Rothbaum (front, left), holding Johnny (then called Jan), with Johnny's uncles before the war. Krakow, Poland, circa 1930.

Johnny's father, Schulem Rothbaum, with two of his sisters. Krakow, Poland, circa 1920.

Roman (Romek) Rothbaum, Johnny's older brother, in front of their house on Zamenhofa Street. Krakow, Poland, circa 1938.

1. Johnny's prisoner identity card used by the Germans during the war. The name on the card is Jan Rothbaum and it notes that he is a Polish Jew who has been in Plaszow and Auschwitz concentration camps.
2. Johnny's refugee identification card, issued by the International Refugee Organization Austria. The card notes Johnny's new name, Ephroim (spelled Efroicer) Jablon, and a false birthdate. Documents courtesy of International Tracing Service (ITS) Bad Arolsen.

Johnny Jablon after the war. Austria, 1946.

Johnny and his friend Joe Hefter in the Bindermichl DP camp. Linz, Austria, 1946.

1 Johnny studying electronics in the ORT school. Bindermichl DP camp, Linz, Austria, 1947.
2 Johnny (front) with friends at ORT. In the back row, third from the left, is Johnny's friend Joe Luden; and in the back, second from the right, is his friend Mayer Friedman. Bindermichl DP camp, Linz, Austria, 1947.

1   Johnny with Sylvia Margulies, who organized the ORT school in Bindermichl. Linz, Austria, 1947.
2   Johnny (crouching in front) with friends from ORT, welcoming Sylvia Margulies. Linz, Austria, 1947.

1   Johnny (far right) with friends on the ship *General Langfitt* on their way to Canada. September, 1948.
2   Johnny (front row, third from the left) on the *General Langfitt* with his friends Joe Luden and Mayer Friedman (back row) and Charlotte Wolf. September, 1948.

1   Johnny on Mount Royal. Montreal, 1949.
2   Johnny (in back) with his friends in Montreal, 1949.
3   Johnny (right) with his friends Joe Luden (left) and Mayer Friedman (centre). Montreal, 1949.

1–4 Johnny and his fiancée, Sally Pancer. Montreal, circa 1951.

Johnny and Sally with friends at their wedding. Montreal, January 20, 1953.

Johnny outside his business, Magic Touch TV Sales & Service. Montreal, 1954.

1 Johnny and his business partner, Alex Kurzman, inside their store. Montreal, 1954.
2 Johnny working in his store. Montreal, 1954.

1   Johnny and his daughter, Debbie, on her wedding day. Montreal, 1995.
2   Johnny and his grandson, Daniel. Montreal, 2017.
3   Johnny and Debbie. Montreal, 2016.
4   Johnny's daughter, Debbie, his grandson, Daniel, and his son-in-law, Jack. Montreal, 2014.

1 Johnny on his return to his childhood home on Zamenhofa Street, seventy-five years after the war, as part of the educational tour March of the Living. Johnny is holding a photo of his brother on a bicycle in the same spot before the war. Krakow, Poland, 2018. Photo credit: Naomi Wise.
2 Johnny with others from the March of the Living in front of the barracks at the Auschwitz-Birkenau Memorial and Museum. Oświęcim, Poland, 2018. Photo credit: PBL Photography.

1 Johnny at the Tykocin synagogue, where he celebrated his bar mitzvah with the March of the Living. Tykocin, Poland, 2018. Photo credit: PBL Photography.
2 Johnny at the Tykocin synagogue, during his bar mitzvah ceremony. Tykocin, Poland, 2018. Photo credit: PBL Photography.

Index

Ada (daughter of Raisel Shal), 6, 17, 28, 30, 32, 36
Aktion, xxiii, 93, 94
aliyah, 5, 62, 65, 81
Allied forces, 114, 115. *See also* American forces; British forces
Am Yisrael Chai, 59
American forces, 94, 122, 124–25
American Jewish Joint Distribution Committee (JDC), xxv
Angel of Death. *See* Mengele, Dr.
antisemitism, xxv, 13–14
Appell, 104, 106
Appellplatz, 40, 42, 45–46, 97–98, 99, 104–5, 106, 109, 110
Auschwitz, xxiii, 39, 44, 48, 64, 94, 101, 103–10, 111, 113, 150
Automatic Laundries Limited (Toronto), 75
bar mitzvah, 22–23, 80–82, 151
barracks leaders, 45–46
Bellalis family, 72
Bełżec camp, xxi, xviin5, 32, 36, 93
Bergen-Belsen concentration camp, xxiv, 49–51, 55

Bergen-Belsen displaced persons (DP) camp, 55–67
Bergen-Hohne training area, 60–61
Betar movement, 13, 61
Beth David Synagogue (Toronto), 77
Beth Radom Synagogue (Toronto), 77, 79
bimah (raised platform in synagogue), 11
Bimko, Dr., 56
Bindermichl (Austria), 127
Birkenau, 103, 150
Birnenbaum, Richard, 79
birzha (underground currency exchange), 20
Blitzer, Dave, 137, 141
Blockältester (block elder), 104, 113
Blockschreiber (block secretary), 109
B'nai Radom (Sons of Radom), 76–77
Bogomolny (school friend of Sam), 11–12
Bolesław, Mr., 107, 108, 109, 110
Bornstein, Lilka, 11–12

Bremerhaven (Germany), 69
British forces, 53–57, 65
British Mandate Palestine, xvi, xxvi, 5–6, 12, 62, 65, 93
British police, 62
Brühand, Benny, 33–34, 35, 39
Brühand, Yechiel (uncle of Sam), 6, 14–15, 19, 28, 30, 31, 32, 33, 39, 44
Bürstenbinderei, 39, 42, 44
Bürstenfabrik factory, 39–40
Canada, 130
Canadian Jewish Congress (CJC), xxvi, xxvii, 130, 131, 133, 136, 138
Cantina 46, 60, 61
Canton (Ohio), 70–74
cantors, 11, 73, 77
cattle cars, 22, 33, 45
Central Committee of Liberated Jews, xxv, 56, 59
Central Tracing Office (International Tracing Service), xxv
Chapnick, Lemek, 11–12
Chorzów (Poland), xvi, 6–9, 10–15, 79
Chumash (Torah), 11
crematoria, 105, 106, 107, 108, 110–11
Cyrankiewicz, Józef, 107–8
Czortków (Chortkiv, in Ukraine), 19
Daniel (grandson of Johnny), 152
David (barracks leader), 49–50
Dawes Road Cemetery (Toronto), 76–77
death marches, xxiv, 31, 49, 111, 116, 119–20

Deerfield Beach (Florida), 125
Displaced Persons (DP) camp (Wels), 124–31
VIII British Corps, 53–54
Elbaum, Adam, 128
11th Armoured Division (British forces), 53–54
Emalia (enamel) factory, xxiii, 95
Emanuel (cousin of Johnny), 90–91
Erenwort, Rutka, 11–12
Esterka of Poland, 11
Ethiopia, 91
Exodus, 65
Falkenberg camp, xxiv, 46–49, 72
Finkelstein (Jewish police lieutenant), 43
First Polish Republic, XVIII
Fisher, Miss, 136, 137, 138
Flantzbaum brothers, 67
forced marches, 49, 111–12, 116, 119
Friedman, Mayer, 137, 141
gabbai (assistant to rabbi), 22
Gajer, Akiva (paternal uncle of Sam), 5, 10
Gajer, Anshel (paternal uncle of Sam), 5, 10
Gajer, Avraham. *See* Weisberg, Sam (Avraham Ichak Gajer)
Gajer, Chaya (paternal aunt of Sam), 5, 10
Gajer, David (paternal uncle of Sam), 5
Gajer, Eli Meyer (father of Sam): in Bergen-Belsen, 49–51; in British Mandate Palestine, xvi, 5–6; in Chorzów, 7–10, 79–80; death,

51, 59; in Falkenberg, 46–49; in Gross-Rosen, xxiii, 45–46; leaving Chorzów, 18–19; in Lwów, 19–24, 27–28; memorial, 76–77; in Plaszow, xxi–xxii, 33–45; in Wolbrom, xx–xxi, 28–32
Gajer, Faige (paternal aunt of Sam), 5, 9
Gajer, Hersh Leib (paternal grandfather of Sam), 9, 10
Gajer, Lika (paternal grandmother of Sam), 9, 10
Gajer, Moshe (brother of Sam), 6, 12
Gajer, Yehezkel Yosef (brother of Sam), 8, 12, 15
Gajer (née Shal), Esther Etel (mother of Sam): during beginning of war, 17–25; in Bełżec, 36; business, 6, 7, 8; childbirth, 6; family illness, 7, 12–13; in Germany, 14; in Lwów, 27–28; marriage, 5–6; memorial, 76; visit to Niemirów, 10; in Wolbrom, 28–32
Galicia, xvii, xviin1, 5, 9, 10
Garfinkel, Isaac, 77
Geller (Jewish police chief), 30–31, 36–37
General Government (in occupied Poland), xvii, xviin4, xviii
General Langfitt, 131–32
German forces, 24, 49, 90, 91, 92, 93, 94, 95, 114–15, 120. *See also* SS
Germany: declaration of war on Soviet Union, 27; invasion of Soviet Union, xvii; invasion/occupation of Poland, xvii–xviii, 14, 18, 19, 90, 152
Gestapo, 94
Glass, Abie, 77
Gniwisch, Pinny, 151
Goldman, Harry, 76, 77
Gordon family, 134
Göth, Amon, 40, 41–43, 45, 46, 64, 99–100, 101
Green, Isaac, 77
Greta (nanny of Sam), xvi, 8, 13
Gross, Dr., 108
Gross, Leon, 98, 101
Grossman, Morris, 74, 75
Grossman, Nathan, 74
Gross-Rosen camp, xxiii, 45–46
Gunskirchen camp, xxiv, 94, 119–20, 122
Gureck (owner of housing complex), 7
Gusen camp, xxiv, 94, 115–16
gymnasium (high school), 29, 89–90
Hako'ach soccer team, 128
Halifax (Nova Scotia), 132–33
HaSharon café (Jerusalem), 5, 82
Hefter, Joe, 124, 127, 130
Herzl Health Centre (Montreal), 133
HIAS (Hebrew Immigrant Aid Society), xxvii, 69
Hilowicz (Jewish police chief), 40, 41
Hitler, Adolf, 7–8, 14, 19, 92
Hoffman, Benny, 77
Hoffman, Edith, 74
Horowitz, Anna, 74
Horowitz, Lily, 74

Horowitz, Rachmiel, 60, 70–71, 73, 74
Horowitz, Susie, 74
Hujar, Albert, 98
Hujowa Górka (Hujar's Hill), 98
Hungarian Jews, 116, 119
Isenberg family, 79, 80
Israel, xxvi, 76, 77, 90–91
Jablon, Debbie (daughter of Johnny), 146, 152
Jablon, Ephroim. *See* Jablon, Johnny (Jan Rothbaum)
Jablon, Johnny (Jan Rothbaum): in Auschwitz, 103–10; bar mitzvah, 151; birth, 89; immigrating to Canada, 131–33; on forced march, 111–12; in Gusen, 115–16; in Krakow, xviii, 89–95; in Linz DP camp, xxiv, 124–31; on March of the Living, 147–52; marriage, 146; in Mauthausen, 112–13, 116–17; in Melk, 113–15; in Montreal, 133–43; name change, 131; in Plaszow, 97–101
Jablon, (née Pancer) Sally (wife of Johnny), 145–46
Jackson's Point (Ontario), 74, 80
Jacobs, Anna, 71–72, 73, 74
Jacobs, Elaine, 72
Jacobs, Morris, 71–72, 74
Jacobs, Ronny, 72
Janic, *Oberwachtmeister*, 34–35
JDC (American Jewish Joint Distribution Committee), xxv
Jerozolimska Road, 33, 41
Jerusalem, 82
Jesin, Aaron (son-in-law of Sam), 83, 84
Jesin, Ahuva Leah (grandchild of Sam), 83, 84
Jesin, Aliza Chaya (grandchild of Sam), 84
Jesin, Maytal Mira (grandchild of Sam), 84
Jesin, Raphael Chaim (grandchild of Sam), 84
Jesin, Shlomo Meir Yirmiyahu (grandchild of Sam), 84
Jesin, Yehezkel Moshe (grandchild of Sam), 84
Jewish Brigade, 62
Jewish Camp Committee, 56
Jewish Council (Judenrat), xviii, xix, 39
Jewish ghetto police, 56–57, 95
Jewish Vocational Services (JVS), 138–39
Joachisman, Dysia, 94–95
Joachisman family, 94–95
Joseph (friend on march), 116–17, 120, 121, 122, 123
Judenfrei (free of Jews), 36
Judenrat (Jewish Council), xviii, xix, 39
Jüdischer Ordnungsdienst; Jewish Order Service (OD), xix, 95
Julag I (Plaszow labour camp), xxi, 33–34, 37, 38
Julag II (Plaszow labour camp), 33–34, 35, 37, 39
Julia (neighbour), 72
Kanada, 110, 113

kapos, 45–46, 49, 103, 105, 114, 115, 116
kapote (long black coat), 9
Katzman, Sam, 79
Kasimir the Great of Poland, 11
Kates, Solly, 77
Katowice (Poland), 12
Katz, Dr., 107, 108
Katz, Isadore, 76
Katz, Tobiasz, 98
Katzman family, 80
Keller, Mrs., 64
ketubah (Jewish marriage contract), 61
Kibbutz Afikim, 66, 82
Kielce (Poland), xxv
kippah (religious skullcap), 9
kittels (white robes), 11
Koch, Lina, 134, 136, 142
Kokoczinsky, Mr. (teacher), 11
komandierovka (permit), 22
Kommandos (work outside camps), 44
Königshütte (Germany), 6
Koperwas, Shia, 76
Kote, Herr, 61
Krakow (Poland): under German occupation, xviii–xix, 90; ghetto, xix–xx, xxiii, 39–40, 91–95, 147; history, 89; Jewish Council, xviii; Jewish district, 11; Johnny's visit, 148–49; pre-war Jewish population, xv, xviii
Krakow-Plaszow *Zwangsarbeitslager*. *See* Plaszow labour camp

Krynica (Poland), 17, 90
Kurzman, Alex, 146
Lanail, Mirele, 138
Lanail, Mr., 138
Lanail, Mrs., 138
Landry, Cantor, 77
Latanski family, 136, 142
Laufer, Berl, 56
Lederman, Gucia, 75
Leibovitch, Bumi, 134
Levy, Rosie, 81–82
Linz (Austria) DP camp, xxiv, 92, 124–31, 145
Lubaczów (Poland), 5
Lubavitchers (members of Orthodox, Hasidic movement), 80
Lublin (Poland), 24–25
Luden, Joe, 129, 130, 133, 134, 135–37
Lutowiska (Galicia), 9–10
Lwów (Poland), xvii–xviii, 19–25, 27–28
Lwów ghetto (Poland), xvii–xviii, xviin5, 27–28
Magic Touch TV Sales & Service (Montreal), 146
Majdanek camp, 93
Malinger (camp survivor), 53
March of the Living, 147–52
Margulies, Sylvia, 129
Mauthausen camp, xxiv, 94, 112–13, 116–17
Melk camp, xxiv, 94, 113–15
Memmingen (Germany), 60–61
Mengele, Dr., 105, 106, 108, 109
Merchant of Venice, The

(Shakespeare), 141
Meyer (cousin of Esther Shal), 8
Michaleros, Tommy, 75
Michaleros, Vera, 75
Miller, *Oberscharführer*, 34, 35–37, 38–39, 40–41
minyan, 22–23
Modern Laundry (Toronto), 74
Montelupich prison (Krakow), 91
Montreal (Quebec), 133–43
Moravská Ostrava (Czechoslovakia), 112
Müller, Franz, 98
Murray (cutter), 139, 140
Narocka, Rosa, 67, 69, 70–71
Niemirów (Poland), 5, 10, 23
NKVD, 21, 64
Nuremberg Trials, 57
Oberlander, Rabbi, 61
OD (Jüdischer Ordnungsdienst; Jewish Order Service), 95
Organisation Todt, 47
ORT (Organization for Rehabilitation Through Training), 57, 128–29, 137
Paluch (brother-in-law of Bela Shal), 28
Pancer, Sally (wife of Johnny), 145–46
Panzertruppenschule, 55
Pasiak (striped prisoner clothing), 46, 104, 105, 109
Pauline (survivor liaison), 147, 149, 151
payot (sidelocks), 43
Peggy (survivor liaison), 147, 151

Pier 21 (Halifax), 132
Plaszow forced labour and concentration camp, xxn8, xxi, xxiii, 45, 95, 97–101, 149, 150
Poale Zion, 61
Podgórze (Poland), 38
Poland: division, xvi–xvii, 19–20; First Polish Republic, xvin1; General Government, xvii, xviii, xviin4; German invasion/occupation, xvii–xviii, 14, 18, 23, 27, 90, 152; liberation, 49, 53; post-war Jewish population, xxv; Soviet invasion/occupation, xvi, 14, 18, 19, 22, 23, 90, 152
Polish Blue Police, xx, 24, xxn7
Polish forces, 18–19
Polish police, xx, 24, xxn7
Polish-Lithuanian Commonwealth, 7
politruk (military official), 21–22
Poslushny, Chaim, 56
Potok, Mr., 61
Price, Dr., 47–48
Promenade Builders, 79
Racibórz (Poland), 112
Radom (Poland), 76, 77
Radomer Society (Toronto), 76
Rakoff, Cantor, 73
Rakoff, Mrs., 73
Red Cross, 128
Reimer, Mr., 131, 133, 134, 141
Reiter, Diana, 99
Revier, 98
Roma, 109, 115
Romania, 19

Rosen, Abie, 77
Rosenbaum, Henry, 76, 77
Rosenbaum, Sam, 77
Rosensaft, Josef (Yosele), 56, 59, 63
Rothbaum, Jan. *See* Jablon, Johnny (Jan Rothbaum)
Rothbaum, Joseph (brother of Johnny), 89, 94
Rothbaum, Roman (Romek; brother of Johnny), 89, 90, 91, 92, 93, 94, 95
Rothbaum, Schulem (father of Johnny), 89, 91, 92, 94, 95, 107
Rothbaum (née Ormian), Dora (mother of Johnny), 89, 93–94, 95
Rozenzweig, Ahuva, 81
Rozenzweig, Avraham, 81
Rozia (maternal aunt of Johnny), 90
Sally (aunt of Johnny), 94
Saltzman, Srulik, 39–40
Saltzman brothers, 39–40
Schecter, Meyer, 28
Schindler, Oskar, xxiii, 95
Schindler's List, 41–42
Sefer Torah, 22, 23
Segrams, Mabel, 71
selections, 43, 103, 105, 108
Shal, Esther Etel. *See* Gajer (née Shal), Esther Etel (mother of Sam)
Shal, Raisel (maternal aunt of Sam), 5, 6, 28, 30, 31, 36
Shal, Shaiva (maternal aunt of Sam), 5, 6, 7–8, 14–15, 17, 28, 30, 31, 32, 36

sheitls (wigs), 6, 66
shtiebl (small Orthodox synagogue), 11
Siberia, xvii, 22–23, 63, 64, 145
Silberman, Mr., 81
Silberman, Mrs., 81
Sir George Williams University (Concordia University), 137–38, 141, 146
Sisters of Mercy, 123
Słomniki (Poland), 37, 38
socialism, 20–21
Sonderkommando, 110
Soviet forces, xxiii, 19
Soviet POWs, 113–14, 115
Soviet Union: German declaration of war, 27; German invasion, xvii; invasion/occupation of Poland, xvi–xvii, 14, 18, 19, 90, 152; liberation of Poland, 49; refugee resettlement, 22
Spiegler, (née Shal), Bela (maternal aunt of Sam), 5–6, 12, 14–15, 17–18, 19–20, 22, 23, 63–66, 73, 80, 82–83
Spiegler, Avraham (cousin of Sam), 18, 19–20, 22, 23, 63–64, 66, 73, 81, 82
Spiegler, Chaim (cousin of Sam), 18, 19–20, 22, 23, 63–64, 66, 73
Spiegler, Moshe (uncle of Sam), 6, 12, 14–15, 17–18, 19, 20, 22, 23
Spiegler, Ruth, 82
Spielberg Brothers orchestra, 127
SS, 31–32, 35, 43–44, 45–46, 47, 48, 93, 94, 98, 103–4, 105, 112

SS *Muriel*, 69, 70
Stalin, Joseph, 17, 20
Stan Vine Construction, 79–80
Star of David, xviii, 24, 27, 38, 91, 92, 105
Steinbaum, Lola, 61, 73
Steinbaum, Monia, 60, 73
Steinbaum, Rachmiel, 60, 73
Steinberg, Chana (née Schecter), 19
Steinberg, Duszia, 19
Steinberg, Meyer, 19
Sternberg (camp survivor), 53
Stubenälteste (room leader), 107
Stubendienst (house worker), 35
Szyf, Max, 100, 134
tallit (prayer shawl), 23
tefillin (phylacteries), 23, 82
Teperman family, 82
Toronto (Ontario), 74–77
Treblinka, 93
Trepman, Paul, 56
Tully, Lynda, 84
Tykocin (Poland), 151
tzedakah (charitable kindness), 23
Ukrainian guards, 34–35, 42, 97, 98, 100
uncle of Johnny, 128–29
United Nations Relief and Rehabilitation Administration (UNRRA), xxiv, 57
US forces, 94, 122, 124–25
USAT *General Stuart Heintzelman*, 69–70
Vilnick, Mr., 57
Vine, Stan, 79–80
Wajsberg, Samek, 67, 69, 70–71

War of Independence (Israel), 65
war orphans, xxiv, 131
Warsaw (Poland), 150–51
Wasseralfingen (Bavaria), 63
Weinberg, Leo, 59–60, 61
Weinberg, Luba, 60, 61
Weisberg, Rosa (née Bronka Horowitz; wife of Sam): in Canada, 74–77, 79–80; in Canton, Ohio, 71–74; children, 73, 75; in DP camp, 56, 57, 60, 67; immigrating, 69–71; in Israel, 80–82; marriage, 60, 71
Weisberg, Estelle Sharon (Esther Shaiva; daughter of Sam), 73, 75–76, 80, 82, 83, 84
Weisberg, Sam (Avraham Ichak Gajer): bar mitzvah, 22–23; in Bergen-Belsen, 49–51, 53–57; in Bergen-Belsen DP camp, xxiv, 59–67; birth, 7; in Canada, 74–77, 79–80; in Canton, Ohio, 70–74; children, 73, 75; in Chorzów, xvi, 6–9, 10–15; in Falkenberg camp, 46–49; in Gross-Rosen, xxiii, 45–46; in Israel, 80–82; in Lublin, 24–25; in Lwów, xvii, 19–23, 25, 27–28; marriage, 60, 71; in Plaszow, xxi–xxii, 33–45; in Wolbrom, xx–xxi, 28–32
Weisberg, Stanley Max (Shlomo Meyer; son of Sam), 75–76, 80, 83-84
Weistrich, Ernest, 11–12
Wels (Austria), 123–31

Wieliczka (Poland), xix–xx, 18, 28, 33, 44
Wiesenthal, Simon, 128
Wilzek, Mr., 37–38
Wise, Naomi, 148
Wolbrom (Poland), xx–xxi, xxn6, xxii, 28–32, 36–37
Wolf, Charlotte, 134, 136
Wolkesh, Eddie, 75
World Federation of Bergen-Belsen Survivors, 56
Yanina (housekeeper), 8, 12
Yosele (cousin of Esther Shal), 10
Yosele (Falkenberg inmate), 48–49, 72
Young Pioneers, 21
Zelker family, 72
Zionism, 65
Zionists, xxvi, 5, 13, 57, 61
Zolty, Yumek, 56, 57

The Azrieli Foundation was established in 1989 to realize and extend the philanthropic vision of David J. Azrieli, C.M., C.Q., M.Arch. The Foundation's mission is to support a wide spectrum of initiatives in education and research. The Azrieli Foundation is an active supporter of programs in the fields of education, the education of architects, scientific and medical research, and the arts. The Azrieli Foundation's many initiatives include: the Holocaust Survivor Memoirs Program, which collects, preserves, publishes and distributes the written memoirs of survivors in Canada; the Azrieli Institute for Educational Empowerment, an innovative program successfully working to keep at-risk youth in school; the Azrieli Fellows Program, which promotes academic excellence and leadership on the graduate level at Israeli universities; the Azrieli Music Project, which celebrates and fosters the creation of high-quality new Jewish orchestral music; and the Azrieli Neurodevelopmental Research Program, which supports advanced research on neurodevelopmental disorders, particularly Fragile X and Autism Spectrum Disorders.